The Ultimate Healthy Dehydrator Cookbook

THE
ULTIMATE HEALTHY
Dehydrator
Cookbook

150 RECIPES TO MAKE AND
COOK WITH DEHYDRATED FOODS

Pamela Ellgen

SONOMA
PRESS

Quick Start Guide

Whether you have several pounds of fresh produce glistening on your kitchen counter or an epic backpacking trip to prepare for, chances are you picked up this book so you could get started dehydrating right away. I share your enthusiasm!

Turn to **page 15** for the **TOP EIGHT REASONS** I love dehydrating—from saving money and reducing food waste to eating locally and concentrating natural flavors.

Next, flip to **page 21** to learn about **DEHYDRATION METHODS** and which one is best suited to your situation.

Turn to **page 27** for all the **TOOLS AND EQUIPMENT** you need to dehydrate safely and efficiently.

For basic recipes for dehydrating **FRUIT**, **VEGETABLES**, **NUTS**, and **HERBS**, turn to part 2, which begins on **page 45**. Part 3 (**page 101**) offers slightly more intricate recipes for **FRUIT LEATHERS**, **JERKY**, **SNACKS**, **RAW VEGAN FOODS**, and even **COMPLETE MEALS** you can make in your dehydrator.

So what do you do with all this tasty food you've prepared? That's the subject of part 4 (**page 149**), which has more than **60 RECIPES UTILIZING DEHYDRATED FOODS**.

*To Brad and Cole, my favorite people
to prepare snacks for and my ultimate
inspiration to eat healthfully.*

Contents

Introduction 8

PART ONE Dehydration Education 11
   CHAPTER ONE Introduction to Dehydration 13
   CHAPTER TWO The Dehydrator's Kitchen 25
   CHAPTER THREE Your First Batch 31

PART TWO Simple Dehydrated Food 43
   CHAPTER FOUR Dehydrated Fruits & Nuts 45
   CHAPTER FIVE Dehydrated Vegetables & Herbs 71

PART THREE Dehydrated Food Recipes 101
   CHAPTER SIX Dried Meats & Jerkies 103
   CHAPTER SEVEN Snacks 115
   CHAPTER EIGHT Raw Foods 131

PART FOUR Recipes with Dehydrated Ingredients 149
   CHAPTER NINE Breakfast 151
   CHAPTER TEN Soups 167
   CHAPTER ELEVEN Vegetarian & Vegan Entrées 185
   CHAPTER TWELVE Meat & Poultry Entrées 203
   CHAPTER THIRTEEN Desserts 225

The Dirty Dozen & The Clean Fifteen 241
Measurement Conversion Tables 242
References 243
Food & Equipment 244
Recipe Index 245
Index 247
Acknowledgments 251
About the Author 252

Introduction

"There are few things that make us feel so positively domestic as putting food in store. I feel I'm putting down roots, laying down a part of the foundation for living."

—Nigella Lawson

Is there anything quite as satisfying as making edibles from scratch? It provides a sense of empowerment. Some of my absolute favorite do-it-yourself food projects emerge from my dehydrator. From homemade banana chips and fruit leathers to grass-fed beef jerky and gourmet herb blends, the seemingly endless range of items fulfills my desire to create—with an undeniably delicious side benefit of having healthy foods that feed both my creative soul and my family.

I purchased my first dehydrator as an adult while exploring the raw foods. But my real start with dehydrating foods came as a young child. My mom owned a large box dehydrator that she placed in the laundry room on top of the clothes dryer. It hummed along all day and night filled with the abundance from our garden and fruit trees—apples, pears, apricots, and blackberry leathers were my favorites. She also made banana chips that were sweet and chewy—unlike any I found in the market after I left home. An insatiable desire to make these wonderful dried foods remained with me until I plugged in my first dehydrator.

Dehydrating is a cinch to master. Most recipes require fewer than five ingredients, sometimes only one, and less than five minutes of preparation. Simply prepare the food, put it into the dehydrator, oven, or under the sun, and wait. Okay, the waiting isn't always easy. I may or may not have a slight problem with reaching in before the food has finished drying to sneak a bite! I still adore raw foods, but since have expanded my dehydrating repertoire to preparing healthy desserts, preserving fresh fruits and vegetables from my local farmers' market, and making healthy snacks for my two boys.

I'm not the first one to think drying foods is totally brilliant—dehydrating is one of the oldest known food-preservation techniques. Archaeological records indicate that humans have been drying foods for thousands of years, and sun drying was the obvious choice. Early cultures even without consistent sunlight built their own dehydrators to dry everything from fish and meat to fruit and hops. Many of the foods we cook with and enjoy today are prepared according to those early methods, such as raisins, beans, jerky, and seaweed.

If early humans can do it, so can you—and you don't even have to invest in a dehydrator if you don't want to. Outdoor drying presents an economical and environmentally friendly option, especially if you live in a dry climate with plentiful sunshine. The flavor of sun-dried foods may be even better than what you can produce in your home dehydrator. Alternatively, your kitchen oven, especially if it's a convection oven, can be used to dry foods. This book offers suggestions for all these methods.

The reasons for dehydrating food are as compelling today as they were thousands of years ago. It is an environmentally sustainable and simple method of food preservation—much easier than canning or freezing food. It also allows you to save food for times of scarcity. Sure, you could run to the grocery store for tomatoes in the dead of winter, but it's much more fun—and tasty—to just reach into your cupboard. Imagine the taste of summer-fresh tomatoes when your summer garden is just a memory—or apples, peaches, and strawberries. You can have seasonal foods year-round.

This book is brimming with recipes for drying foods and for using many of the delicious dried foods you've made. So, let's get to it by first learning about dehydration itself.

PART ONE

DEHYDRATION EDUCATION

CHAPTER ONE
Introduction to Dehydration

CHAPTER TWO
The Dehydrator's Kitchen

CHAPTER THREE
Your First Batch

Introduction to Dehydration

Before you begin drying foods, it's helpful to know a few things about how dehydrating works, the various methods of dehydration and their advantages and disadvantages, and how dehydration affects the nutritional qualities of food. This chapter covers these topics, after starting with a brief history of food drying techniques dating back to the dawn of the agricultural revolution and up to modern day methods.

A Brief History of Drying Food

Food dehydration is as old as civilization itself. For humans to settle in one geographic region, we needed a way to ensure a consistent food supply year-round. Food preservation was our meal ticket, so to speak. Before the advent of modern technologies, such as electricity and refrigeration, dehydration kept food safe for consumption long after it would have spoiled.

Archaeologists discovered early evidence of food dehydration in the Middle East and Asia from approximately 12,000 BCE. At that time, people used the sun to dry food. Around the same time, people living in what is now Jordan began drying and storing grain in large silos. Grain cultivation, dehydration, and storage continued throughout the region and were a prominent part of ancient Egyptian civilization. Dehydrated foods also allowed for a nomadic lifestyle and exploration. Mongolian explorers lived off dried dairy products as they traveled west on their way to Europe.

Dehydrating also played a significant role in Native American food preservation. Throughout North America, berries, tomatoes, corn, and meats were dried in the sun while plentiful, and stored for consumption during the winter. Pawnee and Wichita tribes in what is now Kansas dried strips of pumpkin and wove them into mats for storage and trade. People living in the highlands of Peru during the pre-Columbian era also dried food in the sun, and discovered that first freezing it overnight in the cold Andes Mountains sped up the drying process the next day.

Throughout history, dehydration has served as more than simply a method of food preservation. Ancient Greeks and Romans enjoyed dried grapes and figs as a delicacy. In Southeast Asia, dried fish and shrimp became dietary staples that brought unmistakable umami (meaty or savory) flavors to many dishes, and still do to this day. In fact, many foods we enjoy today exist because they were originally dehydrated as a method of food preservation.

In addition to sun drying to preserve foods, early dehydration methods involved smoke, salt, wind, and even burying food underground. These methods were mostly pragmatic, and they had their limitations. Precipitation, unpredictable humidity and temperature, and pests made natural food preservation challenging if not impossible at times. In addition, many foods spoiled despite the best efforts. Contemporary food science indicates that some of these early methods left food vulnerable to potential pathogens that could cause illness.

Although modern drying methods involving electric dehydrators and convection ovens lack the poetic charm and energy efficiency of natural dehydration, they certainly accelerate the drying process and ensure uniform results. Nevertheless, whenever possible this book provides sun-drying options.

Why I Love Dehydrating

Of all the food preservation methods—canning, freezing, smoking, pickling, curing, and fermenting—dehydrating is my favorite. Canning, the usual choice for DIY food preservation, requires a lot of hands-on effort cooking food and processing jars to high temperatures. (Is it just me or is handling hot glass and large pots of boiling water just a little intimidating?) But dehydration is simple, easy, and approachable. There are many reasons to love dehydrating.

SAVES MONEY

If you have ever purchased kale chips from the health food store, you don't need any convincing— dehydrating food at home saves major bucks. Vegan fruit and nut bars, granola, beef jerky, and other dehydrated snacks are all a fraction of the cost when you make them yourself instead of buying them.

ALLOWS EATING LOCALLY YEAR-ROUND

When I read Barbara Kingsolver's book *Animal, Vegetable, Miracle*, I was mesmerized by her adventure of eating locally for a year. But none of it would have been possible without food preservation. Although I don't always restrict my food to what has been grown locally, dehydrating allows me to come close. Supporting the environment and having better tasting foods are just two of the benefits of eating local.

What is the shelf life of dehydrated food?

Shelf life depends on whether the food was properly dehydrated and whether it was pretreated. Conditioning dried foods before you store them will even out the moisture content for longer shelf life. Also, keeping dried food in airtight containers away from light and heat will extend their shelf life.

As a general rule, properly dehydrated and stored foods can be saved for about one year, until the season for the fresh variety comes around again. For example, tomatoes dried in late August can be saved into the following summer. The key is thorough dehydration and proper storage. If a stored dried food looks or smells "off," do not eat it.

CONTRIBUTES TO EMERGENCY READINESS

I live on the San Andreas Fault in California and have an emergency preparedness kit ready for "the Big One" to hit. In addition to major natural disasters, relatively small incidents such as tap water contamination and power outages make clean, ready-to-eat food a potential lifesaver—no can opener, washing, or heating required.

EXTENDS SHELF LIFE FOR FOODS

Preserved foods last longer than fresh foods. My husband, Rich, used to joke that eggplant would shudder when I purchased it because it was guaranteed to go bad before I used it. And indeed, that used to be true. After discovering how delicious dehydrated eggplant is, I have liberated myself from the rather short shelf life of eggplant. And the same goes for most fresh produce—if you cannot use it in time, pop it in the dehydrator and use it later, on your timeline.

REDUCES WASTE

Avid gardeners say, "It's zucchini season—don't look your neighbor in the eye!" And as I tended our garden last summer, I understood what they meant. The abundance of zucchini was overwhelming. Whether you're dealing with your own bountiful harvest or simply a sale on produce at your local grocery store, dehydrating allows you to keep food from spoiling and save it for later—no need to doorbell-ditch zucchini on your neighbor's front porch.

EASY TO TRANSPORT

Backpackers know what early explorers did—dehydrated foods weigh less than fresh foods while still retaining their macronutrients. You also don't risk bruising or squashing dehydrated foods. Whether you're hiking the Pacific Crest Trail or accompanying a toddler on a long flight, dehydrated foods are perfect for traveling.

Are dehydrated foods healthy?

Dried foods are naturally low in fat, but they are a concentrated source of sugar—especially fruit—and easy to overindulge in. If you're watching your weight, keep portion sizes in perspective. A small handful of dried banana chips is equivalent to an entire piece of fruit. Also, make sure to drink plenty of water when you eat dried snacks.

CONTROLS SUGAR AND ADDITIVES

Dehydrating food allows you to preserve it without adding copious amounts of sugar, salt, or artificial preservatives, which are often found in commercially prepared canned or smoked foods. Dried foods are also naturally low in fat because fat increases spoilage—so meats must be trimmed of all visible fat.

CONCENTRATES FLAVORS

Raw food chef, restaurateur, and cookbook author Sarma Melngailis wishes there were another word for "dehydrating" and argues that dehydrators should be called "flavor concentrators." I wholeheartedly agree about how delicious dehydrated foods can be. They're loaded with flavor. Just think about the concentrated flavor in sun-dried tomatoes!

HOMEMADE SAVINGS

Saving money through DIY food preparation projects is somewhat of a game to me. I feel a sense of accomplishment when I can skip the packaged food and prepare something myself for a fraction of the cost. This is especially true of dehydrated foods because they have such a long shelf life, ensuring they don't spoil before I intend to use them. Homemade dehydrated foods often taste better than commercially prepared versions, and they don't result in a bunch of packaging being dumped into landfills. A bonus—dehydrating is good for your budget:

$4.79	HAIL MERRY PURE VANILLA MACAROONS	COCONUT MACAROONS (PAGE 125)	$0.50
$9.99	NAVITAS POWER SNACKS	BASIC ENERGY BARS (PAGE 122)	$1.75
$5.99	TRADER JOE'S ORGANIC BEEF JERKY	CLASSIC BEEF JERKY (PAGE 104)	$1.50
$6.99	RAW FOOD CENTRAL CURT'S CLASSIC KALE CHIPS	DRIED KALE (PAGE 89)	$0.50

How Dehydration Works

Food preservation, in general, works by removing, denaturing, or preventing the growth of bacteria, fungi, and other microorganisms that lead to food spoilage. Sugar, salt, and high or low temperatures used in a variety of food preservation methods all facilitate this effect. Dehydrating is slightly different in that it starves bacteria by removing as much moisture as possible. The rate and efficacy of dehydration for food preservation is influenced by several key factors.

TIME

If you think slow cooking is slow, dehydrating is even slower. This came as somewhat of a surprise to me when I started dehydrating. Because you're not actually cooking the foods with your dehydrator, the process takes several hours, if not a full day, for most foods. During the initial 1 to 2 hours of dehydrating, a significant amount of moisture is released from the food and fills the air within the dehydrator. As the moist air escapes, more moisture can evaporate from the food. It is a process that cannot be rushed, so plan ahead and allow a day or two.

TEMPERATURE

Different foods need to be dehydrated at different temperatures. The first dehydrator I purchased heated to one temperature only, about 165°F. All of the food was hot to the touch when it came out of the dehydrator and had crisp, even brittle, exteriors and still moist interiors—an undesirable combination for many food items. When I upgraded to a box-style dehydrator with different temperature settings, I reduced the processing temperature and gained improved texture with greatly increased dehydrating times.

Delicate herbs dry best and retain the most flavor when dried at very low temperatures, around 105°F. Drying temperatures less than 115°F produce the lowest nutrient losses and keep plant enzymes intact for these items, but increase the total length of time to thoroughly dry them. For vegetables, 125°F is recommended so the vegetable's exterior doesn't harden and prevent the interior moisture from evaporating; in fact, dehydrating veggies at a high temperature can actually slow the drying process. Fruits do best at 135°F. High temperatures, 145° to 165°F, are necessary for meat in order to prevent spoilage during the process.

What foods cannot be dehydrated?

Foods that are high in fat, such as milk, eggs, cheese, and butter, are difficult to dehydrate properly in a way that makes them either safe for storage or pleasing to eat. Commercially prepared dried milk powder is made using a spray drier that vaporizes the liquid and dries it quickly using hot gas, which is, clearly, outside the scope of your home dehydrator.

AIRFLOW AND VENTILATION

Airflow and ventilation are essential for successful food dehydration. Early food preservation methods involved open-air drying that in some ways improved dehydration because moisture was wicked away by the breeze and did not "steam" the food within an enclosed space. Box-style dehydrators have the best circulation and ventilation because air flows evenly from the back of the machine out toward the front instead of circulating from the bottom tray up through the machine of stackable-style dehydrators. This is also what makes oven drying challenging—there is no air circulation or air escape unless you have a convection oven and/or prop the door open. Silicone mats or fruit-leather trays impede airflow and ventilation, which can increase drying time. Use them during processing only when they're needed to prevent sticking. When placing food pieces on the dehydrator trays, always leave space between them for optimal air flow.

RAW MATERIAL PREPARATION

If there is ever a time to be precise with measurements it is when you're preparing food to dehydrate. Even a difference of $\frac{1}{8}$ inch in thickness can result in an hour or more difference in food drying time. When preparing food, you want to ensure that the greatest possible surface area is exposed and cut food into uniform sizes. You may even want to use a ruler.

HOW DOES DEHYDRATION AFFECT NUTRIENTS?

Food dehydration decreases the micronutrients in most foods, though not nearly as much as canning or other cooking methods do. The nutrients most affected by dehydration are water-soluble vitamins, particularly vitamin C and, to a lesser extent, B vitamins. However, minerals and fat-soluble vitamins, such as vitamin A, are mostly retained.

There are several ways you can reduce nutrient losses when dehydrating. The first is to dehydrate food at low temperatures. Temperatures lower than 135°F have been shown to preserve enzymatic activity in plants. In addition, to mitigate mineral losses, retain the soaking liquid when rehydrating vegetables or fruit. Fruit soaking liquid can be blended into smoothies, and vegetable soaking liquid can be added to soups, vegetable broths, or used for cooking rice.

Pretreating food before it is dehydrated prevents the loss of some nutrients while increasing the loss of others, and so it is not recommended as a strategy for retaining nutrients.

An overlooked nutrient in food dehydration is the primary element you're trying to minimize: water. When consuming dried fruits, vegetables, and snacks, it is vital to increase your water consumption, because these dried foods do not contribute to your daily hydration needs like they would have in their fresh, whole form. Sufficient water intake also helps improve nutrient absorption from the dehydrated foods you consume.

Dehydration Methods

There's more than one way to remove moisture from food. Just look at traditional methods of drying—you can hang food from a line to blow dry in the wind or even wrap it in a palm leaf and bury it in the sand. As nostalgic as those methods are, this book concerns itself with the three conventional modern methods you're most likely to try: sun drying, oven drying, and an electric dehydrator.

SUN DRYING

The relatively long, slow process of sun drying—days versus hours—produces delicious results. But some climates are better suited to sun drying than others. I have lived in the Pacific Northwest and Arizona—the Northwest being inhospitable to outdoor dehydrating in all but a few hot summer weeks and Arizona drying food almost as quickly in the summer as an electric dehydrator. If you live in a place with high humidity, low temperatures, or intermittent sunlight, sun drying can be difficult if not impossible. A simple rule of thumb is that day temperatures should be 90°F with less than 60 percent humidity for successful sun drying.

Part of the challenge of dehydrating is removing moisture quickly before food spoils. *The low acidity in vegetables makes them unfit for sun drying because they do not dry quickly enough.* Also, sun-dried foods should be pasteurized, through heat or freezing, to prevent spoilage from possible insect larvae.

To dry food in the sun, spread it out on food-grade mesh screens and cover it with sheer mesh cloth to protect it from pests. Check food periodically while it is sun drying to ensure the mesh continues to cover it and to stir or flip the food. Overnight, bring the food indoors to prevent it from reabsorbing moisture.

OVEN AND CONVECTION OVEN DRYING

Before you purchase your first dehydrator, you may want to use your oven to test-dry a few batches of food. I used this test method before investing in an inexpensive stackable dehydrator. The conventional oven provides a uniform low temperature but lacks air circulation and ventilation. Two ways to address this are to prop the oven open an inch or two and to place a fan near the oven door.

The downsides to conventional oven drying are: it takes longer than using an electric dehydrator, it is energy inefficient, and it is somewhat of a hassle. Results can mimic those of an electric dehydrator if you use a convection oven, which circulates air around the food. Set the oven to the same temperature you would use with an electric dehydrator and only dry small batches.

ELECTRIC FOOD DEHYDRATOR DRYING

Electric food dehydrators produce consistently uniform results with minimal energy output. The energy cost of most electric dehydrators is less than 10 cents per hour, depending on the energy costs where you live and the kilowatts of your dehydrator.

Dehydrators and the Raw Food Diet

In my twenties, I became very interested in the raw food movement after meeting and interviewing Ani Phyo, a well-known raw food chef. She simply glowed with radiance, looking more than a decade younger than her real age. It was all the evidence I needed to give it a try, and the plethora of vibrant, delicious ingredients made the foray into raw foods a delight!

WHAT IS A RAW FOOD DIET?

The raw food diet includes fruits, vegetables, nuts, seeds, and oils that have not been heated over 118°F. It typically does not include animal products of any kind, though some raw foodists do consume sushi or, rarely, raw meat.

The rationale for the raw food diet includes these ideas: Minimally processed plant foods have been shown to contribute to health and longevity and to contain antioxidants, enzymes, vitamins, and minerals. Cooking food denatures enzymes, can destroy micronutrients, and can create harmful by-products, especially at high heat. The raw food diet seeks to eliminate these effects for the purest, healthiest food possible.

THE RAW FOOD "OVEN"

Many raw food recipes utilize the dehydrator to heat food gently over a prolonged period while maintaining its nutritional value. The Fudgy Chocolate-Cherry Brownies (page 146) are not only warmed by the dehydrator but also develop a firmer consistency resembling traditional brownies made in an oven. The Basic Nut Crackers (page 133) begin as a loose, spreadable batter and become crisp in the dehydrator.

Most raw food recipes using a dehydrator call for setting the temperature to 118°F or less to retain plant enzymes. Research by the late Dr. John Whitaker, Professor Emeritus, Food Science and Technology, at the University of California Davis, however, indicates that enzymes remain intact at dehydrator settings as high as 140°F.

FAMILY TIME

My two boys love joining me in the kitchen, but they're still too young to use the stove safely and without close supervision. The dehydrator allows us to make yummy, healthy snacks together safely. It's also offers a great opportunity for them to practice their culinary creativity, like combining various fruits to make fruit leather, without fear of failure. It's really satisfying to see them already involved in preparing healthy foods and enjoying nature's candy.

RAW FOOD INGREDIENTS

Raw food recipes may seem intimidating at first. I have tried to keep the ingredients as simple and obtainable as possible—the kinds of foods you probably already eat anyway. All fruits and vegetables are included in a raw food menu. Nuts and seeds also comprise a significant portion of raw recipes. To improve digestion, most nuts are soaked in fresh water for several hours and then thoroughly rinsed to remove enzyme inhibitors. Cold-pressed oils and raw sweeteners are also used. Although technically, maple syrup is not raw, I use it in some recipes. If you prefer a strict raw diet, use raw agave or raw honey (not vegan) instead.

One ingredient you may not be as familiar with is young coconut. It is an off-white color on the outside, not to be confused with mature coconuts covered with a brown, hairy bark. Young coconut is challenging to work with initially, but, with a good sharp knife and a little determination, your efforts will be rewarded. The soft, barely sweet coconut meat inside can form the basis for raw pastas and can be used to make dairy-free ice cream. A delicious bonus is the sweet coconut water inside, which is far better than canned coconut water.

The Dehydrator's Kitchen

You can get started dehydrating immediately and easily with just a few simple tools that you probably already have in your kitchen. But if you love gadgets, you'll also find many clever tools that make food dehydrating easier. Whatever you decide, remember, dehydrating is one of the oldest and simplest food preservation methods around and is designed for you to accomplish with little more than food, air, and sunshine.

The Right Dehydrator

Electric dehydrators are available in two main styles:

Each has advantages and disadvantages, but any model from the cheapest stackable model to the large-capacity box unit will get the job done. When I am going to purchase a new appliance, I like to get the cheapest model (slow cooker, juicer, dehydrator, hand mixer, etc.) to see if I'm going to enjoy using it, and then when my needs exceed its capacity, I upgrade to a model with greater functionality.

A round, stackable tray dehydrator circulates air from the top or bottom of the unit through all of the trays. Additional trays can be purchased later for greater capacity. The round model takes up a small amount of counter space, making them ideal for small kitchens.

One disadvantage of the round stackable models is evident when making desserts, pasta, or crackers when a square surface area is desirable. But, with a little creativity, this feature can be easily overcome. Another disadvantage of this model is that the air circulation and ventilation are less efficient than in the box models, so trays need to be rotated during the drying process.

A box- or cabinet-style dehydrator is often considered superior to the stackable model because air circulates from the back of the unit freely between the trays. And because of its square corners, this model allows you to use square silicone mats for making fruit leather and other spreadable batters.

Whether you choose a stackable or box-style dehydrator, choose one with a thermostat that lets you set the exact temperature desired and a timer that will turn the machine off at the designated time.

Essential Tools and Equipment

I believe the only things you absolutely need to get started dehydrating are a *sharp chef's knife* and a *good dehydrator*. Also, the following tools are helpful:

* **BLENDER** A blender is necessary for making fruit leathers and other spreadable purées for dehydrating. You can either use a countertop or immersion-style blender. I prefer a countertop blender for coconut and nut-based purées.

* **MANDOLINE OR FOOD PROCESSOR** For uniform thickness in vegetables, you may wish to use a mandoline or food processor fitted with a slicing blade.

* **MESH SCREENS AND TRAYS** If you're drying food in the sun, you should invest in food-grade mesh screen material that can be stretched over untreated wood. Or, you can purchase trays already fitted with food-grade mesh screen material. Additional mesh of the same kind should be draped over the food you are drying to prevent debris and insects from spoiling the food.

* **PARAFLEXX OR SILICONE MATS** To make fruit leathers and crackers, use silicone mats for box-style dehydrators or plastic trays for round stackable models. The mats reduce airflow and ventilation so dehydrating takes longer, but they prevent loose batters from dripping through the holes in mesh screen trays.

* **RULER** While not essential, a ruler can help ensure that all food is cut or spread out to the same thickness so that you obtain uniform results.

CLEANING YOUR DEHYDRATOR

Unlike cooking utensils, pots, and pans, your dehydrator trays and screens are very easy to clean. Always consult the manufacturer's manual for specific cleaning instructions.

Trays from box-style dehydrators and stackable models are typically labeled "dishwasher safe." However, I prefer to hand wash both the trays and mats with warm water and mild soap and allow them to air dry before returning them to the machine. Silicone mats should be wiped clean but not soaked. To clean the interior of any dehydrator, sweep debris from the bottom and wipe clean with a damp cloth.

Which herbs are best to dehydrate?

I find that rosemary, thyme, and oregano retain their flavor better than other herbs when dried. More delicate herbs such as basil, cilantro, and dill can be dehydrated but they pale in comparison to the fresh versions.

❈ **SPICE GRINDER** A spare coffee grinder or mortar and pestle both work well for grinding herbs and spices.

❈ **VEGETABLE PEELER** If you prefer that your dehydrated fruit or vegetables are peeled, a vegetable peeler is usually easier to use than a paring knife.

Storage Supplies

Once you have processed all this magnificent dehydrated food, what should you do with it? Well, for starters, you need to keep it dehydrated by storing it in an airtight container. Think about cookies or other dry, crisp baked goods left out overnight; they tend to become limp after absorbing the moisture in the air. They should also be kept away from light and heat, which speed spoilage and nutrient loss. These considerations are important for short-term storage and they are vital for long-term storage—anything beyond the current season.

Following are a few tools and supplies to use in storing your dehydrated foods:

❈ **AIRTIGHT CONTAINERS** Because dried foods are naturally small and light-weight, you may choose zip-top plastic bags, which can be easily tucked into small cupboards. I prefer to use glass instead of plastic, and I love using mason jars, which can be used again and again. In addition, you can use a vacuum-sealing machine to preserve the freshness and texture of dried foods.

❈ **LABELS** If you're storing food for longer than one season, or if you have ground a food into a powder, labels can make them easier to identify.

❈ **SILICA GEL PACKETS** Packaged desiccants, such as silica gel, can be used to absorb potential moisture from inside the container once it is sealed. Use small packets marked as "food safe" (safe to use with foods) though they are inedible.

SEASONAL GARDENING FOR YEAR-ROUND ENJOYMENT

Many gardeners approach food dehydrating as a way to preserve the abundance in their garden. But thinking in the reverse direction also works: Begin with the dehydrator in mind and plant a garden. Following are some plants that are easy to grow and delicious when dehydrated:

Herbs The best herbs to dehydrate are perennials with woody stems, such as thyme, lavender, and rosemary. They're great for the home gardener, too, because if planted and cared for, one plant will last for many years if not indefinitely, depending on the climate in your region.

Peppers Both bell peppers and hot chile peppers are easy to dehydrate and can be added to a variety of savory dishes. Pepper plants are not difficult to grow, but they are sensitive to temperature. Consult a gardening manual for information on cultivating peppers and other fruits and vegetables.

Tomatoes My favorite plants to grow are tomatoes. The heady fragrance of their stems and juicy sweetness of the fruit are worth the weeks of waiting as the seeds grow from tiny sprouts to towering plants. I like to purchase or save heirloom seeds for tomato varieties that I'm not likely to find in the grocery store. Roma tomatoes are my favorite for halving and dehydrating. Plant at least six plants in your garden if you intend to enjoy them fresh and have some left over for dehydrating.

Zucchini After you make zucchini bread, the best solution for dealing with an abundance of zucchini is to dehydrate it. If you're new to gardening, make sure to space zucchini plants far from one another, as they tend to get big. Also, harvest vegetables before they get big—which can happen quickly so check your plants daily. Pick zucchini when they are 4 to 5 inches long for the best flavor and texture.

Your First Batch

If you have skipped ahead to this section, I totally get it. Dehydrating is fun and you want to get started right away! There's very little that can go wrong with dehydrating. The process is so forgiving—if you under-dehydrate something, just pop it back into the dehydrator to continue drying. Nevertheless, here are a few essential tips to ensure success with your first batch.

What To Dehydrate

When I began gardening, I visited a garden store to purchase plants and was wisely advised to plant the foods I wanted to eat. This is simple but sound advice and I think it translates well to dehydrating—dry the foods you want to eat.

Some of the easiest foods to begin with are those that require no pretreatment and are enjoyable to eat out of hand. Chapters 4 and 5 include single-ingredient recipes for dehydrating fruits and vegetables. In addition to being the easiest foods to dry when you are just getting started, their uses are also virtually endless. Some of my personal favorites for first-time dehydrating are:

- Apples
- Bananas
- Kale
- Peaches
- Pears
- Peppers
- Tomatoes

When selecting food to dehydrate, remember that the dehydrator concentrates flavors. In other words, the flavors present in the fresh food item will be intensified in the dried version. Vegetables and fruit should be ripe but not overripe, and free from blemishes or bruising. But don't toss out bruised produce; simply cut away the bad spots. Avoid dehydrating foods high in fat, such as avocados, or that also have an overpowering, unctuous flavor, such as olives. Fat contributes to spoilage and intense flavors are further intensified.

Prep Work Pointers

While dehydrating doesn't require the same level of care and attention as cooking or canning, it does involve thoughtful preparation. Proper washing, peeling, slicing, pretreating, and sanitary handling practices can make or break your food dehydrating adventure. Following is a general guide to preparing food for dehydration (for specific instructions, see each individual recipe).

PITTING, PEELING, AND CHECKING

Many fruits, such as mangos, plums, peaches, and cherries, contain inedible peels and/or pits. You should discard these before you begin dehydrating because both impede the release of moisture from the fruit. Removing pits from stone fruits can be done with special tools. With cherries, I prefer to cut them in half to remove the pit because it speeds drying time.

Typically, vegetables can be dehydrated with their skins intact, but some have coarse skin that should be peeled, such as garlic, ginger, carrots, sweet potatoes, and the woody ends of asparagus.

Some fruits, such as grapes and blueberries, have taut skins that must be "checked" before dehydrating—essentially, just breaking the fruit's skin to allow moisture to be released. You can do this by blanching the fruit in boiling water for 30 to 60 seconds and then shocking it in an ice water bath; the skin will split. Or, simply run a serrated knife over the fruit gently, allowing the teeth of the knife to puncture the skin, causing it to split.

CUTTING AND SLICING

You need both a chef's knife and a paring knife for dehydrating. The most important thing to remember when cutting food for dehydrating is to cut it in uniform pieces with the end use in mind: Do you want to grind it into a powder, layer it into a casserole, or simply enjoy as a snack? The answer should determine the cut size and shape. Foods should also be cut to expose the greatest surface area in order for moisture to evaporate. This is particularly important with foods that remain unpeeled.

Learning to love my chef's knife was one of the best things that happened to my arsenal of cooking skills. Hold the chef's knife in your dominant hand pinching the blade between your thumb and index finger. Place the tip of the knife on the cutting board, bisecting the space diagonally. Hold the food in your opposite hand with your fingers tucked underneath your palm. The knife should move as if it is an extension of your forearm as you slice.

FOOD SAFETY

Ensure proper sanitation in your kitchen while dehydrating foods, especially when handling raw meat. Consider watching an online food handler's video to familiarize yourself with safe food handling procedures. Following are a few general guidelines to observe.

Keep prepared foods and meats below 40°F or above 140°F. Anywhere between this range is considered the "danger zone" in which bacteria multiply rapidly. Meat should be dehydrated at 145° to 165°F to keep it out of this range.

Arrange meat and poultry at the bottom of your refrigerator and in glass or metal trays to catch any juices that could contaminate ready-to-eat foods.

Designate separate cutting boards for raw meat and fresh produce to reduce the likelihood of cross-contamination. This is especially important when dehydrating fruits and vegetables because you're drying at temperatures in the middle of the danger zone. If these foods have come in contact with juices from raw meat, you're creating a bacterial playground in the dehydrator and increasing risk of foodborne illness.

Clean and sanitize knives, cutting boards, and utensils between uses, especially after handling raw meat. Create a sanitizing solution by mixing 1 tablespoon of bleach to 1 gallon of water. Do not change the ratio; it will become unsafe if the amount of bleach is increased or ineffective if decreased.

SEVEN TIPS FOR SUCCESS THE FIRST TIME

1. Plan ahead. How much surface area do you have on your dehydrator trays or on your oven racks or sun-drying trays? Consider the size and shape of the food you will be dehydrating after it is cut to make sure it covers the trays but leaves space for air to circulate.

2. Choose carefully. Dehydrate the kinds of food you know you'll enjoy eating and that don't require pretreatment. You'll enjoy hassle-free preparation and be sure to love the results. Success the first time will give you the confidence to venture into dehydrating foods that require a bit more preparation.

3. Prepare evenly. In a batch of food to be dried, each food piece should be cut in the same size and shape to allow for even drying. Food pieces should be placed on the trays so that the greatest surface area is exposed, allowing moisture to escape. Leave space between food pieces.

4. Allow time. Give yourself at least twenty-four hours for your first batch, especially if you're using an oven. (Plan for several days if you are sun drying.) It most likely won't take a full twenty-four hours, but planning on that amount of time may help you resist the temptation to pull the food out early for a nibble.

5. Allow space. Your dehydrator needs space around it for airflow. Make sure it is not pushed up against any walls or placed in a humid environment.

6. Cool it. Remove a few pieces of food from the dehydrator and allow them to cool on the countertop before testing for doneness. They will stiffen as they cool and you will get a better understanding of whether they are done or need more time.

7. Store carefully. Put thoroughly dried food into sealed, labeled containers, and store in a cool, dry, dark place.

Perfect Pretreatment

Pretreating foods before dehydrating reduces the risk of bacterial contamination, increases shelf life, improves texture and appearance, and often improves taste. Pretreatment options include blanching and shocking, freezing, roasting, and soaking in water, acidulated water, or a sugar solution.

Each method has its advantages and disadvantages, and, while none is essential to food dehydration, especially for short-term storage, modern food science confirms that pretreating reduces the risk of foodborne illness.

Dipping in a sulfur solution is another option for pretreatment, but I suggest it only occasionally because sulfuric compounds may cause allergic reactions in some individuals.

BLANCHING AND SHOCKING

Blanching and shocking are procedures often used for vegetables to inhibit bacterial growth and improve the texture of the finished dried food. Blanching involves plunging prepared food into boiling water for up to 3 minutes and then plunging it into an ice water bath to stop the cooking process (shocking). The food is then patted dry thoroughly before placing it on dehydrator trays.

Steaming food in a steamer basket for up to 3 minutes accomplishes a similar effect and may reduce nutrient losses.

Syrup blanching is typically used for fruits, particularly cranberries and other fruits that have low sugar content. It improves the texture of most fruits, making them softer and more pliable when dry. Syrup blanching uses 1 part sugar and 1 part corn syrup to 2 parts water and follows the method for traditional blanching. However, *do not* shock the food in ice water after cooking; simply drain thoroughly and spread on dehydrator trays.

ACIDULATED WATER SOAKING

Treating food with some form of acid before dehydrating lowers the pH, inhibiting growth of microorganisms, and it also reduces browning in some foods, such as potatoes, apples, pears, and bananas. Optional acids include citrus juice, citric acid powder, and ascorbic acid. Other acidic liquids such as pineapple juice or vinegar may be diluted with water and used, but those impart unwanted flavors.

Alternatively, you can spray foods with undiluted lemon juice before dehydrating. Use the following formulas to prepare acidulated water and soak foods for up to 5 minutes before patting dry and dehydrating:

❖ $\frac{1}{4}$ cup lemon juice to 2 cups water
❖ 1 teaspoon citric acid powder to 2 cups water
❖ 2 teaspoons ascorbic acid to 2 cups water

SUGAR SOAKING

As its name suggests, sugar soaking involves dipping and soaking food in a simple sugar syrup. It can improve the taste, texture, appearance, and shelf stability of fruits. I prefer to use natural fruit juice or honey instead of refined sugar for sugar soaking. You may also choose evaporated cane juice, agave, or maple syrup. Use the following formulas to create a simple syrup and soak for 2 to 3 minutes before draining thoroughly and dehydrating:

❖ 2 cups undiluted fruit juice, such as pineapple or orange juice
❖ $\frac{1}{4}$ cup honey dissolved in 2 cups warm water
❖ $\frac{1}{4}$ cup sugar dissolved in 2 cups warm water

Drying Time

The range of drying times provided for many dehydrated foods varies widely. There are several reasons for this range because many factors affect how quickly a food dries, especially water content, sugar content, size, surface area, and humidity in the atmosphere on the day you dehydrate.

WATER CONTENT

Foods begin with varying percentages of water content. Even the same types of foods can have differing water content depending on their variety and the time of day and year they were harvested. In general, meats contain 60 to 70 percent water and fruits and vegetables contain 80 to 95 percent.

SUGAR CONTENT

The sugar content of foods increases drying time, which should be considered if you're soaking fruit in a sugar solution before drying. Nevertheless, sugar acts as a preservative, and so sweet foods do not need to be crisp-dry for them to be safe for storage.

Can you dehydrate different types of food simultaneously?

It is best to choose foods with similar dehydrating temperature and time requirements, such as vegetables with other vegetables and leafy greens with other greens or herbs. Also keep in mind that the aroma of some foods is quite pungent and may affect the flavor of other foods in the dehydrator. For example, I prefer to dehydrate garlic and onions with other savory foods.

SIZE AND SURFACE AREA

Smaller pieces of food with greater surface area dry more quickly than larger pieces of food. To speed drying time, cut foods in small, uniform pieces. They should be spread on trays to allow for air to circulate between them. A crowded dehydrator will slow drying time.

HUMIDITY

The air in the atmosphere has an impact on the foods inside your dehydrator. The dehydrator constantly circulates air from outside the unit to the inside, where the humidity rises, air escapes, and fresh "unhumidified" air replaces it. Although you have no control over the weather and atmosphere, you can choose to dehydrate on dry days and refrain from cooking liquids uncovered on your stove.

Average Drying Times

	DEHYDRATOR	OVEN	SUN
Fruits	10 to 20 hours	15 to 25 hours	3 to 4 days
Vegetables	4 to 8 hours	6 to 12 hours	not recommended
Herbs	3 to 4 hours	4 to 6 hours	1 day
Meats	4 to 8 hours	8 to 12 hours	not recommended
Fruit leathers	6 to 10 hours	10 to 15 hours	3 to 4 days
Crackers	4 to 6 hours	6 to 10 hours	not recommended

How Do You Know It's Done?

With such widely varying drying times, it is helpful to know what to look for when evaluating dehydrated food for doneness. Food that will be consumed quickly, such as trail mix for your backpacking trip the following weekend, does not need to be thoroughly dry. However, food that you intend to store beyond the week must be impeccably dried and properly stored to keep it safe and delicious. Here are a few general guidelines for evaluating a food's doneness. Consult individual recipes for specific criteria.

* **Vegetables** will be crisp and airy.
* **Fruit** will be leathery and slightly pliable.
* **Herbs** will be crisp and crushable.
* **Meat** will be semi-hard and leathery.

Conditioning

Even uniform preparations can yield uneven results; some food pieces in a batch will be dry while others will retain a small amount of moisture. Conditioning takes four or five days, but, if done properly, will extend the shelf life of your dried foods. Simply place all the dehydrated and thoroughly cooled food into glass or plastic jars, filling them about two-thirds full. Cover and put in a cool, dry place. Gently shake the jars once a day. The moisture content will even out over the entire batch. If beads of condensation form on the inside of the jar, the food pieces are emitting moisture, so return the entire batch of food to the dehydrator for another two to four hours, depending on the type of food and its thickness.

What To Do with Dehydrated Foods

Now we're getting to the fun part—what to do with all your delicious dehydrated foods. The options are virtually endless, especially if you have properly prepared and packaged the food for long-term storage. Here are just a few convenient and delicious uses.

EAT IT

The first option, perhaps the most obvious, is to just eat it! Dried fruits and nuts, beef jerky, and trail mix are delicious and traditional dried snacks, but vegetables can be pretty tasty, too. For example, dried root vegetables make crispy chips for snacking and dipping.

GRIND INTO POWDER

I love pulverizing dehydrated foods into a powder. The powders are not only an inexpensive alternative to commercially prepared versions but also liven up many dishes I might never have thought to add them to. You can easily grind dried leafy greens, such as kale and spinach, into a green drink powder. I enjoy grinding mushrooms into a powder to coat roasts with or stir into Mushroom & Pea Risotto (page 188). The dried food must be really dry and crisp to grind easily.

Dehydrated foods can also be used in cooking in the same way you might use the fresh food. Most foods should be rehydrated first, but with moist cooking methods, such as soups and sauces, the rehydration can occur during cooking. Dried fruit is delicious in sweet desserts or as a stuffing for meat. A variety of dried vegetables can be combined for healthy soup mixes.

Rehydrating Foods

Some dehydrated foods rehydrate better than others, but few return to their original state when rehydrated. Nevertheless, most can be rehydrated and used in cooking or applications in which texture is less important. Dried corn and tomatoes are delicious in soups. Dried mushrooms work beautifully in risotto, and dried apples can be rehydrated to make pie or crisp.

To rehydrate dried foods, place them in a heat-proof container. Pour water over the food to fully cover. You can use boiling water for faster results, but you will lose some nutrients in the process. Cold-water soaking typically takes several hours and the food should be refrigerated while it rehydrates.

One of my favorite ways to rehydrate dried foods is with liquids other than water, such as broth or wine. For example, dates rehydrated in espresso and maple syrup is delicious over ice cream. Or dried figs soaked in orange juice and Grand Marnier is exquisite as a dessert or spooned over waffles.

TROUBLESHOOTING

The outside of food is hard, but the inside is still moist. This occurs often with vegetables that have been dehydrated at higher temperatures. Lower the temperature to 125°F, or even to 115°F, and prolong the drying time.

The food feels tacky. Sometimes food that is first soaked in a sugar solution will feel slightly tacky when placing it into the dehydrator, but this effect should disappear when it is properly dried. If food still feels sticky, continue drying for another hour or more.

The food is too crisp. If you accidentally overdry something you intend to eat out of hand and it is brittle and difficult to chew, simply set it on a plate, uncovered, and allow it to absorb moisture from the air.

The food dries unevenly, despite careful preparation. Rotate dehydrator trays 180 degrees for more uniform drying. Remove pieces that dry first and allow the remaining pieces to continue drying.

Fruit leather sticks to the mat. If you spread fruit leather too thin, it will be difficult to remove from the mat without tearing. The problem occurs with parchment paper, as well—the fruit and the paper become inseparable. The solution is to spread the fruit leather to at least ⅛ inch in the center and as much as ¼ inch thick at the edges.

PART TWO

SIMPLE DEHYDRATED FOOD

CHAPTER FOUR
Dehydrated Fruits & Nuts

CHAPTER FIVE
Dehydrated Vegetables & Herbs

Dehydrated Fruits & Nuts

Apples 46

Apricots 47

Bananas 48

Blueberries 50

Cherries 51

Citrus Fruits 52

Coconut 53

Cranberries 54

Dates 55

Figs 56

Grapes 57

Kiwis 58

Mangos 59

Melon 60

Nectarines
& Peaches 61

Nuts & Seeds 62

Pears 64

Pineapple 65

Plums 66

Raspberries 67

Rhubarb 68

Strawberries 69

Apples

YIELD 1 quart ✤ PREP TIME 10 minutes ✤ PRETREATMENT lemon juice

Having grown up in the Northwest, I have enjoyed many batches of dried apples. I remember peeking into the dehydrator to see if they were done and sneaking one or two slices before they were completely dry. Dehydrated apples are perfect lightweight snacks for hiking and camping, and are useful in savory dishes, such as the Cream of Celery Soup (page 175). They are delicious in sweet desserts such as Apple-Thyme Compote in Pinot Noir (page 227). If you enjoy the texture and added fiber, leave the apples unpeeled.

2 to 3 pounds apples, washed and peeled

1. Cut each apple into 8 wedges and arrange on the dehydrator tray. Spray with lemon juice.

2. Dehydrate until still pliable or completely crisp and no moisture remains.

SUN	OVEN	DEHYDRATOR
2 to 4 days	135°F, 8 to 10 hours	135°F, 6 to 8 hours

PER SERVING (¼ CUP) CALORIES: 44; FAT: 0G; CARBS: 12G; SUGAR: 9G; FIBER: 2G; PROTEIN: 0G; SODIUM: 1MG

Apricots

YIELD 1½ cups ❋ PREP TIME 5 minutes, plus 5 minutes inactive time
PRETREATMENT sulfite solution

Look for ripe California-grown apricots during the peak growing season (between April and July). I love using dried apricots in Moroccan dishes or just eat them as a simple snack. They're also delicious chopped and added to granola. Unless they are pretreated with sulfur, apricots will brown naturally when dried.

1 pound apricots, washed, halved vertically, and pitted

1. Soak the apricot halves in the sulfite solution for 5 minutes. Drain and pat dry.
2. Place the apricots cut-side up on dehydrator trays. Dehydrate for 8 hours and flip, placing them cut-side down on the tray. Continue drying for another 6 to 8 hours until soft and leathery and no moisture remains.

SUN	OVEN	DEHYDRATOR
3 days	not recommended	135°F, 14 to 16 hours

PER SERVING (¼ CUP) CALORIES: 36; FAT: 1G; CARBS: 8G; SUGAR: 6G; FIBER: 2G; PROTEIN: 1G; SODIUM: 1MG

Bananas

YIELD 4 cups ❊ PREP TIME 5 minutes ❊ PRETREATMENT none

Purchased dried bananas have almost nothing to do with the deliciously chewy, sweet, dried bananas you can prepare in a home dehydrator. I love mixing dried bananas with roasted peanuts and chocolate chips for a delicious trail mix. They're also great to stuff into my kids' lunch sacks without worrying they'll turn to mush by lunchtime.

15 ripe bananas, peeled and cut crosswise into ½-inch-thick slices

1. Divide the banana slices among the dehydrator trays.

2. Dry for 10 to 12 hours or until the edges are slightly crisp and the interior is chewy but not moist.

SUN	OVEN	DEHYDRATOR
2 to 4 days	135°F, 12 to 18 hours	135°F, 10 to 12 hours

PER SERVING (¼ CUP) CALORIES: 98; FAT: 0G; CARBS: 25G; SUGAR: 14G; FIBER: 3G; PROTEIN: 1G; SODIUM: 1MG

Blueberries

YIELD 1 cup ✳ PREP TIME 10 minutes ✳ PRETREATMENT blanch or freeze (optional)

The sweet flavor of summer is available year-round in preserved blueberries. They're delicious added to granola and yogurt or stirred into Vegan Blueberry-Apple Muffins (page 155). Drying is my favorite method for preserving blueberries, though you must break the skin to allow moisture to escape.

1 pound fresh blueberries, rinsed, sorted, stemmed, and patted dry

1. Blanch or freeze berries before drying. Spread berries on a dehydrator tray. Gently run a sharp serrated knife over the berries in a sawing motion. The weight of the blade should be sufficient to break the skin of several berries. Repeat over the whole tray.

2. Dry until the berries have shrunk and are soft and chewy.

SUN	OVEN	DEHYDRATOR
5 to 7 days (do not pretreat)	135°F, 15 to 18 hours	135°F, 10 to 15 hours

PER SERVING (¼ CUP) CALORIES: 65; FAT: 0G; CARBS: 16G; SUGAR: 11G; FIBER: 3G; PROTEIN: 1G; SODIUM: 1MG

Cherries

YIELD 2 cups ❖ PREP TIME 10 minutes ❖ PRETREATMENT none

Dried cherries are mouth-puckering tart and sugary sweet with a complex mineral element, all at the same time—like cherries, only more so. They're delicious added to trail mix, granola, or rehydrated in savory cooking.

2 pounds fresh cherries, stemmed, rinsed, and patted dry

1. With a paring knife, halve the cherries and remove the pits.
2. Spread the cherries on the dehydrator trays. Dry until flat and leathery.

SUN	OVEN	DEHYDRATOR
2 days	135°F, 12 to 18 hours	135°F, 10 to 15 hours

PER SERVING (¼ CUP) CALORIES: 17; FAT: 0G; CARBS: 18G; SUGAR: 15G; FIBER: 2G; PROTEIN: 1G; SODIUM: 0MG

Citus Fruits

YIELD 2 cups fruit, 1 cup zest ❈ PREP TIME 10 minutes ❈ PRETREATMENT none

I lived in Arizona for a few years and was undone by the abundance of citrus fruit growing there—nearly every home had one or two citrus trees in its yard. As much as I love grapefruit, oranges, and lemons, I simply could not eat enough to feel as if I'd "squeezed" the most out of the season. Dehydrated citrus is surprisingly delicious, producing a sweet, sour, chewy bite. Use dried grapefruit and oranges for a snack or to garnish salads, and use the peel to flavor mulled wine or cider and to add brightness to savory dishes.

2 pounds citrus fruit, washed

1. With a sharp knife, remove the zest (outer layer of peel) in long, thin strips, avoiding the white pith. Set the strips on a dehydrator tray and dry until brittle.

2. Cut the top and bottom off each fruit, set on one end, and remove any remaining peel and pith so the fruit is exposed. For larger fruits, such as grapefruit and orange, use a paring knife to cut along the sides of the membranes to release the segments. For smaller fruits, such as lemons or limes, slice in half horizontally.

3. If you prefer to leave the peel intact, cut the fruit horizontally in ¼-inch-thick slices and place on the dehydrator tray.

4. Place the citrus pieces on a separate dehydrator tray. Dry until the fruit is soft and leathery but no moisture remains.

SUN	OVEN	DEHYDRATOR
2 to 3 days for fruit; 1 day for zest	135°F, 8 to 12 hours, or more, for fruit; 4 to 6 hours for zest	135°F, 10 to 12 hours for fruit; 4 to 6 hours for zest

PER SERVING (¼ CUP) CALORIES: 33; FAT: 0G; CARBS: 11G; SUGAR: 3G; FIBER: 3G; PROTEIN: 1G; SODIUM: 0MG

Coconut

YIELD 1 cup ✻ PREP TIME 10 minutes ✻ PRETREATMENT none

Dehydrating your own coconut may seem like a hassle when it is readily available in the supermarket. But it's nice to skip the sugar found in many commercial coconut varieties. Also, doing it yourself lets you infuse the coconut with other flavors, such as ginger and soy to make a natural vegan "jerky," or sea salt and vanilla for a sweet snack.

1 coconut

1. Poke holes through the "eyes" of the coconut using a clean screwdriver and a hammer, drain the water, and discard it. (Unlike young coconuts, the water in mature coconuts is unappealing to drink.)

2. Using a hammer, crack the coconut into several pieces and run the white parts over a box grater until all the meat is shredded.

3. Spread the grated coconut on a dehydrator tray lined with a silicone mat. Dry until pliable and almost crisp.

SUN	OVEN	DEHYDRATOR
2 to 3 days	135°F, 4 to 6 hours	135°F, 4 to 6 hours

PER SERVING (2 TBSP) CALORIES: 106; FAT: 10G; CARBS: 5G; SUGAR: 2G; FIBER: 3G; PROTEIN: 1G; SODIUM: 6MG

Cranberries

YIELD 1 to 2 cups ❖ PREP TIME 10 minutes ❖ PRETREATMENT simple syrup blanch

I would love to tell you that you can dry cranberries at home without sugar, but unless you have a serious sour tooth, you probably won't enjoy unsweetened, dried cranberries. Nevertheless, you can prepare them with considerably less sugar than commercially prepared varieties. These are delicious in Salted Chocolate Cranberry Bars (page 162) or added to granola and trail mix. They can also be rehydrated easily to make a special meal—the Herb-Crusted Pork Loin with Cranberry Sauce (page 214).

2 quarts water

¼ cup sugar

1 pound cranberries, washed and sorted

1. Prepare an ice-water bath.

2. In a medium saucepan over medium heat, bring the water and sugar (a simple syrup) to a simmer. Add the cranberries and blanch in the syrup for 3 to 5 minutes. Drain and then plunge into the ice-water bath. Drain and pat dry with paper towels.

3. Spread the cranberries on the dehydrator tray. Dry until no moisture remains and the fruits are flat and leathery but still soft.

SUN	OVEN	DEHYDRATOR
2 to 4 days	not recommended	135°F, 15 to 18 hours

PER SERVING (¼ CUP) CALORIES: 31; FAT: 0G; CARBS: 5G; SUGAR: 2G; FIBER: 2G; PROTEIN: 0G; SODIUM: 0MG

Dates

YIELD 1 to 2 cups ❈ PREP TIME 10 minutes ❈ PRETREATMENT none

Fresh dates are already quite sweet because they're loaded with natural fruit sugar. So, if you're looking for a concentrated source of energy, dried dates are it. They're a great addition to trail mix, especially for strenuous outdoor activities such as hiking, climbing, or snowboarding. You can dry the dates whole, or halved and pitted for a quicker drying time. Medjool dates are relatively large and really delicious, but you can use other kinds of dates.

1 pound Medjool dates, halved and pitted

Spread the date halves on dehydrator trays. Dry until shriveled and firm and no moisture remains.

SUN	OVEN	DEHYDRATOR
2 to 3 days	135°F, 10 to 15 hours	135°F, 8 to 10 hours

PER SERVING (1 TBSP) CALORIES: 85; FAT: 1G; CARBS: 22G; SUGAR: 20G; FIBER: 2G; PROTEIN: 1G; SODIUM: 0MG

Figs

YIELD 1 to 2 cups ❃ PREP TIME 10 minutes ❃ PRETREATMENT none

Fig trees abound where I live in California and I love the fruit's grassy, barely sweet earthiness. Dried figs have a slightly different flavor profile, with concentrated sweetness. They are delicious rehydrated in red wine for a sophisticated fruit compote or roughly chopped and added to salads. You can also dry fig leaves, grind to a fine powder, and use in homemade pasta dough or as a crust for roasted chicken.

1 pound figs, rinsed and patted dry

1. Cut the figs vertically into halves or quarters, and remove and discard the stem.

2. Spread the figs cut-side up on the dehydrator tray. Dry until leathery and no moisture remains.

SUN	OVEN	DEHYDRATOR
3 to 4 days	not recommended	135°F, 18 to 24 hours

PER SERVING (2 TBSP) CALORIES: 44; FAT: 0G; CARBS: 10G; SUGAR: 4G; FIBER: 2G; PROTEIN: 0G; SODIUM: 0MG

Grapes

YIELD 2 cups ❋ PREP TIME 10 minutes ❋ PRETREATMENT blanch

Commercially prepared dried grapes, better known as raisins, were called "nature's candy" by marketers in the 1980s. The moniker is never truer than with homemade dried grapes, which are deliciously sweet and free from the sulfites used in preparing many commercially available types. Select seedless varieties and choose organically grown grapes, if possible. If you want to dry them in the sun, leave the grapes on the vine and suspend them from a clothesline or tree branch, making sure to take them in at night.

2 pounds seedless grapes, stemmed and sorted

1. Prepare an ice-water bath.

2. Blanch the grapes in boiling water for 45 to 60 seconds. Drain and then plunge into the ice-water bath. Drain and pat dry with paper towels.

3. Spread the grapes on the dehydrator trays. Dry until flat and wrinkled and no moisture remains.

SUN	OVEN	DEHYDRATOR
3 to 5 days	not recommended	135°F, 20 to 24 hours

PER SERVING (¼ CUP) CALORIES: 76; FAT: 0G; CARBS: 19G; SUGAR: 18G; FIBER: 1G; PROTEIN: 1G; SODIUM: 2MG

Kiwis

YIELD 2 cups ✿ PREP TIME 10 minutes ✿ PRETREATMENT none

Dried kiwi flesh has a beautiful, translucent green hue, very similar to the fresh fruit. Drying intensifies kiwi's natural tartness. It is delicious as a snack eaten out of hand or chopped and added to homemade granola or trail mix for a surprising pop of flavor. The peel becomes tough when dried, so I recommend peeling the fruit before drying it.

2 pounds kiwi fruit, gently rinsed and patted dry

1. Slice the top and bottom off each fruit and discard. Stand the fruit on end and carefully remove the peel with a paring knife, removing as little fruit as possible. Cut the fruit crosswise into ½-inch-thick slices.

2. Spread the kiwi slices on the dehydrator tray. Dry until thin and chewy and no moisture remains.

SUN	OVEN	DEHYDRATOR
2 to 3 days	135°F, 10 to 14 hours	135°F, 8 to 12 hours

PER SERVING (¼ CUP) CALORIES: 69; FAT: 1G; CARBS: 17G; SUGAR: 10G; FIBER: 3G; PROTEIN: 1G; SODIUM: 3MG

Mangos

YIELD 2 cups ✤ PREP TIME 10 minutes ✤ PRETREATMENT none

Dried mango is easily available in most grocery stores, but it usually has been treated with sulfur and the flavor hardly resembles the fresh fruit. Home-dried mango slices are much tastier and are delicious to eat as a snack or rehydrated in the Mango Chutney (page 211).

Cooking spray or vegetable oil   6 fresh mangoes

1. Lightly coat the dehydrator trays with cooking spray or vegetable oil.

2. Stand a mango on its end with its narrow side facing toward you and its "cheeks" (halves) facing to either side. Slice through the fruit about $\frac{1}{4}$ inch off center on each side of the pit. This leaves you with 2 mango "cheeks."

3. Place each mango half skin-side down and cut a checkerboard pattern into the flesh without cutting through the skin. Scoop the chunks out with a spoon.

4. Spread the mango pieces on the dehydrator trays. Dry until flattened and leathery and no moisture remains.

SUN	OVEN	DEHYDRATOR
2 to 4 days	135°F, 12 to 16 hours	135°F, 8 to 12 hours

PER SERVING (¼ CUP) CALORIES: 109; FAT: 1G; CARBS: 26G; SUGAR: 23G; FIBER: 3G; PROTEIN: 1G; SODIUM: 3MG

Melon

YIELD 2 cups ❖ PREP TIME 10 minutes ❖ PRETREATMENT none

Cantaloupe, honeydew, and other muskmelons are sweet and delicious when dried. Watermelon may be dehydrated but, as its name suggests, has an exceptionally high water content, which makes drying times long and the dried watermelon slices are brittle. All melons make tasty snacks. Cantaloupe is delicious rehydrated with vanilla and sugar for a sweet fruit compote.

1 muskmelon, such as honeydew or cantaloupe, halved and seeded

1. Cut the melon into 4 pieces. With a paring knife, remove the rind.
2. Cut each piece into about 4 slices, or whatever size yields $\frac{1}{4}$-inch-thick slices.
3. Place the melon on the dehydrator trays. Dry until still pliable but no moisture remains.

SUN	OVEN	DEHYDRATOR
2 to 4 days	135°F, 12 to 14 hours	135°F, 10 to 12 hours; 18 hours for watermelon

PER SERVING (¼ CUP) CALORIES: 25; FAT: 0G; CARBS: 6G; SUGAR: 5G; FIBER: 1G; PROTEIN: 1G; SODIUM: 6MG

Nectarines & Peaches

YIELD 2 cups ✳ PREP TIME 10 minutes ✳ PRETREATMENT simple syrup blanch

Peaches and nectarines are my absolute favorite stone fruits, especially in summer when purchased from a local farmers' market. The juices drip from the fruit and create a delicious sticky mess. When selecting fruit, look for ripe but still firm fruit; otherwise, they can be difficult to pit. Dried peaches bring back the flavors of summer anytime in Vanilla-Peach Pie (page 231).

2 pounds peaches or nectarines, halved and pitted

2 quarts water

¼ cup sugar

1. Cut the fruit into ½-inch-thick wedges, leaving the peel on.

2. In a large pot over high heat, stir together the water and sugar. Bring to a gentle boil, and turn down the heat to medium. Cook the fruit for 2 minutes. Drain well.

3. Place the fruit on the dehydrator trays. Dry until soft and chewy and no moisture remains.

SUN	OVEN	DEHYDRATOR
3 to 4 days	135°F, 12 to 15 hours	135°F, 8 to 12 hours

PER SERVING (¼ CUP) CALORIES: 68; FAT: 0G; CARBS: 17G; SUGAR: 15G; FIBER: 2G; PROTEIN: 1G; SODIUM: 0MG

Nuts & Seeds

YIELD 4 cups ❁ PREP TIME 10 minutes ❁ PRETREATMENT soaking

Soaking and rinsing nuts and seeds before dehydrating improves their digestibility. The process removes naturally occurring phytates and enzyme inhibitors. Even though cashews and almonds have already been pasteurized, soaking is still recommended before dehydrating. Use dehydrated nuts to make trail mix or granola bars or to simply enjoy out of hand.

4 cups nuts or seeds   12 cups water

1. In a large bowl, cover the nuts with the water. Set aside to soak for at least 4 hours, but no more than 24 hours.

2. Drain the nuts and discard the soaking water. Rinse the nuts in a sieve or colander under cold running water until the water runs clear.

3. If you're drying small seeds, line the dehydrator trays with silicone mats. Spread the nuts on the dehydrator trays. Dry until crispy.

SUN	OVEN	DEHYDRATOR
2 to 4 days	165°F, 4 to 6 hours	135°F, 12 hours

PER SERVING (2 TBSP) CALORIES: 103; FAT: 9G; CARBS: 3G; SUGAR: 1G; FIBER: 2G; PROTEIN: 5G; SODIUM: 3MG

Pears

YIELD 2 to 3 cups ✻ PREP TIME 10 minutes ✻ PRETREATMENT lemon juice

Dried pears are one of my favorite dried fruits. Fresh pear has such a mild, delicate flavor, and drying amps it up for a pleasant natural fruit snack. Dried pears add sweet complexity, featured in the Pork Tenderloin with Stewed Pears (page 216).

2 pounds pears, rinsed and patted dry

1. Cut the pears in half vertically, and remove the stem and core. Cut the halves into ¼-inch-thick slices. Spray with lemon juice.

2. Place on the dehydrator trays. Dry until leathery and no moisture remains.

SUN	OVEN	DEHYDRATOR
2 to 3 days	135°F, 8 to 10 hours	135°F, 8 to 12 hours

PER SERVING (¼ CUP) CALORIES: 66; FAT: 0G; CARBS: 17G; SUGAR: 11G; FIBER: 4G; PROTEIN: 0G; SODIUM: 1MG

Pineapple

YIELD 1 to 2 cups ❖ PREP TIME 10 minutes ❖ PRETREATMENT none

Like dried mango, dried pineapple is easily available in most supermarkets but has been heavily sulfured and sweetened, losing the essence of the fruit. Fortunately, it's easy to dry pineapple at home. Dried pineapple is delicious as a simple snack or as a sweet addition to the Fruity Quinoa Pilaf (page 164).

1 whole pineapple, top and bottom removed

1. Stand the pineapple upright and cut away the rough peel. Cut the pineapple vertically through the core into quarters. Lay each quarter on its side and cut away the core. Cut each wedge into ¼-inch-thick slices.

2. Spread the pineapple slices on the dehydrator trays. Dry until the fruit has shrunk and no moisture remains.

SUN	OVEN	DEHYDRATOR
3 to 4 days	135°F, 10 to 12 hours	135°F, 8 to 10 hours

PER SERVING (¼ CUP) CALORIES: 82; FAT: 0G; CARBS: 22G; SUGAR: 16G; FIBER: 2G; PROTEIN: 1G; SODIUM: 2MG

Plums

YIELD 2 cups ❉ PREP TIME 10 minutes ❉ PRETREATMENT none

"Dried plum" sounds so much better than the alternative "prune." And, these dried plums taste so much better than the sulfured, commercial types. For small, wild plums, leave the pit in. For larger freestone plums, halve the fruit and remove the pit before drying. Dried plums are delicious in Plum Compote (page 226) or rehydrated for a sauce to drizzle over meat.

2 pounds plums, rinsed and patted dry

1. With a paring knife, halve the plums and remove the pits. Invert the plum halves, gently pushing the flesh outward, or cut the halves into ¼-inch-thick slices.

2. Spread the fruit on the dehydrator trays. Dry until leathery and no moisture remains.

SUN	OVEN	DEHYDRATOR
3 to 4 days	135°F, 10 to 14 hours for slices	135°F, 8 to 12 hours for slices; 12 to 18 hours for halves

PER SERVING (¼ CUP) CALORIES: 34; FAT: 0G; CARBS: 9G; SUGAR: 7G; FIBER: 1G; PROTEIN: 1G; SODIUM: 0MG

Raspberries

YIELD 2 cups ❊ PREP TIME 10 minutes ❊ PRETREATMENT none

I grew up eating fresh raspberries straight off the bush. They were always fresh—a nice perk because raspberries tend to spoil quickly. Fortunately, dehydrating fresh raspberries keeps them delicious long after the season has passed. Choose firm, bright-fleshed berries, not soft, dark ones. I love dried raspberries in my morning granola sprinkled over plain yogurt. They're also delicious as a snack.

1 pound raspberries, thoroughly rinsed and drained

1. The crevice in the center of the raspberry has a tendency to hold water, so turn them upside down on a paper towel for a few minutes before placing them in the dehydrator.

2. Spread the berries on the dehydrator trays. Dry until crisp and slightly airy.

SUN	OVEN	DEHYDRATOR
2 to 3 days	135°F, 10 to 12 hours	135°F, 8 to 10 hours

PER SERVING (¼ CUP) CALORIES: 29; FAT: 0G; CARBS: 7G; SUGAR: 3G; FIBER: 4G; PROTEIN: 1G; SODIUM: 1MG

Rhubarb

YIELD 2 cups ❋ PREP TIME 10 minutes ❋ PRETREATMENT none

Dried rhubarb makes a bright, flavorful addition to fruit pies, crisps, and cobblers. It's especially wonderful in the Strawberry-Rhubarb Crisp (page 230). Choose firm, slender stalks for the best taste and texture, avoiding those that are overgrown or wilting. Also, avoid the leaves because they're toxic.

1 pound rhubarb, rinsed and patted dry

1. Cut the rhubarb lengthwise, through each stalk, and then cut into $\frac{1}{4}$-inch dice.

2. Spread the rhubarb on the dehydrator trays. Dry until firm, shrunk, and no moisture remains.

SUN	OVEN	DEHYDRATOR
not recommended	135°F, 8 to 10 hours	135°F, 6 to 8 hours

PER SERVING (¼ CUP) CALORIES: 12; FAT: 0G; CARBS: 3G; SUGAR: 1G; FIBER: 1G; PROTEIN: 1G; SODIUM: 2MG

Strawberries

YIELD 2 cups ❋ PREP TIME 10 minutes ❋ PRETREATMENT none

Fresh strawberries from the farmers' market are a treat for my kids. They're bursting with natural fruit sugars and flavor (which is more than I can say for supermarket strawberries). Dried strawberries make a yummy snack or can be rehydrated to make a delicious strawberry freezer jam.

1 pound strawberries, rinsed and patted dry

1. Remove the stems and hulls from the strawberries. Slice the berries in half vertically.

2. Place the strawberry slices on the dehydrator trays. Dry until leathery and no moisture remains.

SUN	OVEN	DEHYDRATOR
1 to 2 days	135°F, 10 to 12 hours	135°F, 6 to 8 hours

PER SERVING (¼ CUP) CALORIES: 18; FAT: 0G; CARBS: 4G; SUGAR: 3G; FIBER: 1G; PROTEIN: 0G; SODIUM: 1MG

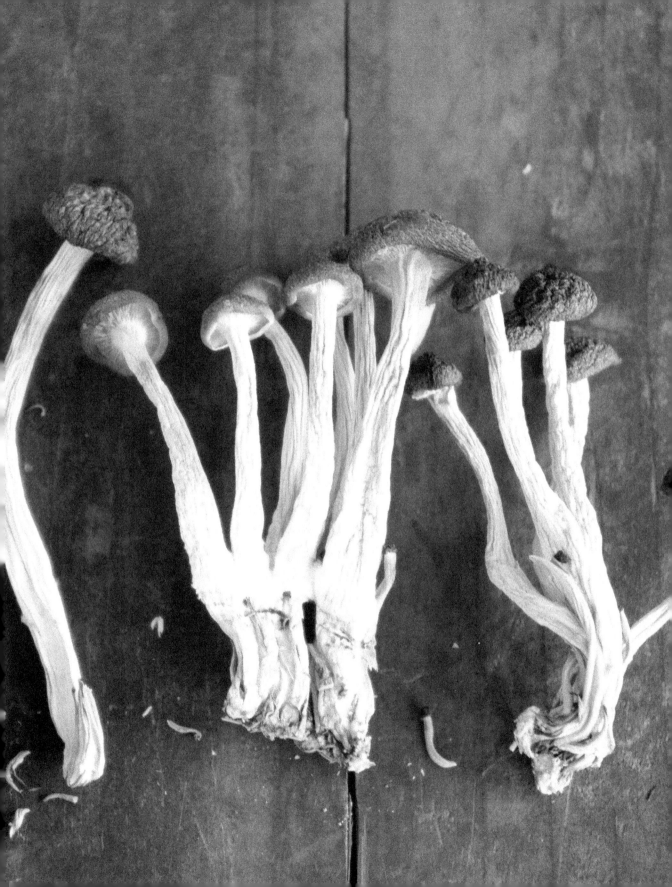

Dehydrated Vegetables & Herbs

Asparagus 72

Beets 73

Broccoli 74

Cabbage 75

Carrots 76

Cauliflower 77

Celery 78

Corn 79

Cucumbers 80

Eggplant 81

Garlic 82

Ginger 83

Green Beans 84

Herbs: Botanical 85

Herbs: Perennial 87

Herbes de Provence 88

Italian Herb Blend 88

Kale & Other Leafy
Greens 89

Leeks 90

Mushrooms 91

Onions 92

Peas 93

Peppers 94

Potatoes 95

Root Vegetables 96

Squash 97

Tomatoes 98

Zucchini 99

Asparagus

YIELD 1 to 2 cups ❖ PREP TIME 10 minutes ❖ PRETREATMENT blanch

Dried asparagus can be used the same way you use fresh asparagus, but it does better when mixed with other ingredients, such as in a casserole, soup, or grain-based dish. It can also be ground into a powder and used to flavor soups and stews. Blanching asparagus ahead of time is vital—don't skip this step!

Sea salt

1 bunch asparagus, woody ends removed and discarded, cut into 1-inch pieces

1. Prepare an ice-water bath and set aside. Bring a large pot of salted water to a boil.

2. Add the asparagus and blanch for 3 minutes. Drain and plunge into the ice water. Drain and blot dry with paper towels.

3. Spread the asparagus on the dehydrator trays. Dry until crisp and inflexible.

OVEN	DEHYDRATOR
125°F, 12 to 14 hours	125°F, 8 to 10 hours

PER SERVING (¼ CUP) CALORIES: 9; FAT: 0G; CARBS: 2G; SUGAR: 1G; FIBER: 1G; PROTEIN: 1G; SODIUM: 16MG

Beets

YIELD 2 cups ❊ PREP TIME 30 minutes ❊ PRETREATMENT steam

I love beet chips for a healthy alternative to fried root vegetable chips. They're a delicious Paleo and vegan-friendly snack. Dried beets can be ground into a powder and used as a natural pink food coloring for baked goods. Don't toss the leaves and stems; they can be chopped and added fresh to salads, or sautéed briefly with garlic for a healthy side dish.

2 bunches beets, thoroughly scrubbed, leaves and stems removed

1. Place the whole beets in a steamer basket in a lidded large saucepan and steam for 20 minutes, or until almost tender. Cool the beets and remove their skins.

2. Cut the beets into thin slices, $\frac{1}{8}$ inch thick to make beet chips, or into $\frac{1}{2}$-inch dice to add to soups and stews, or to make beet powder.

3. Spread the beets on the dehydrator trays. Dry until crisp and no moisture remains.

OVEN	DEHYDRATOR
125°F, 8 to 10 hours for chips;	125°F, 6 to 8 hours for chips;
10 to 14 hours for dice	8 to 12 hours for dice

PER SERVING (¼ CUP) CALORIES: 44; FAT: 0G; CARBS: 10G; SUGAR: 8G; FIBER: 2G; PROTEIN: 2G; SODIUM: 77MG

Broccoli

YIELD 1 to 2 cups ❋ PREP TIME 10 minutes ❋ PRETREATMENT blanch

Dried broccoli florets make an excellent addition to soups and casseroles, or can simply be added to a salad or pasta dish for textural contrast. These are especially delicious in Broccoli-Cheddar Bisque (page 177). Use the dried broccoli stems to make a powder, which can be added to green smoothies or soups.

Sea salt   1 head broccoli, quartered

1. Prepare an ice-water bath and set aside. Bring a large saucepan of salted water to a boil.

2. Add the broccoli and cook for 5 minutes. Drain and plunge into the ice water.

3. Cut the blanched broccoli small florets off the stem, and cut the stem into $\frac{1}{2}$-inch dice.

4. Spread the broccoli pieces onto the dehydrator trays. Dry until crisp and brittle.

OVEN	DEHYDRATOR
125°F, 12 to 14 hours	125°F, 10 to 12 hours

PER SERVING (¼ CUP) CALORIES: 23; FAT: 0G; CARBS: 5G; SUGAR: 1G; FIBER: 2G; PROTEIN: 2G; SODIUM: 38MG

Cabbage

YIELD 2 to 3 cups ❖ PREP TIME 10 minutes ❖ PRETREATMENT blanch

I love the way dried cabbage can be rehydrated in stew and how it takes on all the delicious flavors of a meat's pan juices. Try it with Cabbage & Beef Stew (page 220). You can use any kind of cabbage for dehydrating—red, green, napa, or savoy.

Sea salt

1 head cabbage, cut into ¼-inch slices, core discarded

1. Prepare an ice-water bath and set aside. Bring a large saucepan of salted water to a boil.

2. Add the cabbage and cook for 2 minutes, or until brightly colored. Drain and plunge into the ice water. Drain and pat dry with paper towels.

3. Spread the cabbage on the dehydrator trays. Dry until shriveled and crisp.

OVEN	DEHYDRATOR
125°F, 10 to 14 hours	125°F, 8 to 12 hours

PER SERVING (¼ CUP) CALORIES: 22; FAT: 0G; CARBS: 5G; SUGAR: 3G; FIBER: 2G; PROTEIN: 1G; SODIUM: 0MG

Carrots

YIELD 2 cups ❖ PREP TIME 10 minutes ❖ PRETREATMENT blanch

Dried carrots add flavor to soups and stews. They can also be ground into a fine powder to add to smoothies or shredded for baked goods such as Morning Glory Muffins (page 158). If you plan to shred the carrots, do so ahead of time, skip the blanching pretreatment, and use a silicone mat to prevent the carrot pieces from falling through the dehydrator tray screen.

Sea salt

2 pounds carrots, peeled and cut into ½-inch dice

1. Prepare an ice-water bath and set aside. Bring a large saucepan of salted water to a boil.

2. Add the carrots and cook for 2 to 3 minutes. Drain and plunge into the ice water. Drain and pat dry with paper towels. Alternatively, shred the carrots using the grater attachment of a food processor.

3. Spread the carrots on the dehydrator tray. Dry until crisp.

OVEN	DEHYDRATOR
135°F, 8 to 12 hours	135°F, 6 to 10 hours

PER SERVING (¼ CUP) CALORIES: 46; FAT: 0G; CARBS: 11G; SUGAR: 6G; FIBER: 3G; PROTEIN: 1G; SODIUM: 94MG

Cauliflower

YIELD 2 cups ❖ PREP TIME 10 minutes ❖ PRETREATMENT blanch

Dehydrated cauliflower makes a delicious Creamy Cauliflower Soup (page 179). The dried florets can be rehydrated and the dried stems can be ground into a fine powder. It is especially good with dehydrated roasted Garlic (page 82).

Sea salt   1 head cauliflower

1. Prepare an ice-water bath and set aside. Bring a large saucepan of salted water to a boil.

2. Cut the cauliflower crown into florets and cut the stem into ½-inch dice. Add to the pan and cook for 4 minutes. Drain and plunge into the ice water. Drain and pat dry with paper towels.

3. Spread the cauliflower on the dehydrator tray. Dry until brittle.

OVEN	DEHYDRATOR
125°F, 6 to 8 hours	125°F, 4 to 6 hours

PER SERVING (¼ CUP) CALORIES: 18; FAT: 0G; CARBS: 4G; SUGAR: 2G; FIBER: 2G; PROTEIN: 1G; SODIUM: 37MG

Celery

YIELD 2 to 3 cups ❀ PREP TIME 10 minutes ❀ PRETREATMENT blanch

Celery is a key component of mirepoix (a mixture or rough-cut vegetables, usually onions, carrots, and celery, used for flavoring), a staple in French cooking. Store dried celery with equal parts dried carrots and dried onions for a healthy, flavorful pantry staple. It is also delicious in Cream of Celery Soup (page 175).

Sea salt   1 bunch celery, cut into ½-inch dice

1. Prepare an ice-water bath and set aside. Bring a large saucepan of salted water to a boil.

2. Add the celery and cook for 2 minutes. Drain and plunge into the ice water. Drain and pat dry with paper towels.

3. Spread the celery on the dehydrator tray. Dry until crisp.

OVEN	DEHYDRATOR
125°F, 10 to 12 hours	125°F, 8 to 10 hours

PER SERVING (¼ CUP) CALORIES: 15; FAT: 0G; CARBS: 3G; SUGAR: 1G; FIBER: 2G; PROTEIN: 1G; SODIUM: 92MG

Corn

YIELD 2 to 3 cups * PREP TIME 10 minutes * PRETREATMENT blanch

The versatility of dried corn is amazing. It can be rehydrated and added to soups, stews, and soufflés. Or, you can coarsely grind it for a hearty vegetarian main dish, such as Polenta with Mushrooms (page 190), or grind it finely to make corn tortillas.

Sea salt

12 ears corn, husked and kernels cut from the cob

1. Prepare an ice-water bath and set aside. Bring a large saucepan of salted water to a boil.

2. Add the corn kernels and cook for 2 minutes. Drain and plunge into the ice water. Drain and pat dry with paper towels.

3. Spread the corn on the dehydrator tray lined with a silicone mat. Dry until brittle.

OVEN	DEHYDRATOR
125°F, 10 to 16 hours	125°F, 8 to 10 hours

PER SERVING (¼ CUP)   CALORIES: 88; FAT: 1G; CARBS: 21G; SUGAR: 3G; FIBER: 3G; PROTEIN: 3G; SODIUM: 17MG

Cucumbers

YIELD 2 cups ❋ PREP TIME 10 minutes ❋ PRETREATMENT none

Cucumber chips make a delicious side dish for dipping into hummus or crumbled over green salads. Choose English cucumbers if you can find them (they're typically wrapped in plastic), because they have very small seeds and thin skin.

2 cucumbers, thoroughly washed and patted dry

1. Cut the cucumbers into ¼-inch-thick slices.
2. Spread the cucumbers on the dehydrator trays. Dry until crisp and airy.

OVEN	DEHYDRATOR
135°F, 6 to 8 hours	135°F, 4 to 6 hours

PER SERVING (¼ CUP) CALORIES: 11; FAT: 0G; CARBS: 3G; SUGAR: 1G; FIBER: 0G; PROTEIN: 1G; SODIUM: 2MG

Eggplant

YIELD 2 cups ❖ PREP TIME 5 minutes ❖ PRETREATMENT none

My husband, Rich, always offers his condolences to fresh eggplant entering our house because I can never seem to use it quickly enough before it deteriorates and the seeds turn black. The dehydrator offers a perfect solution. In fact, it actually improves the texture of fresh eggplant by removing excess moisture. Dried eggplant is delicious in Ratatouille (page 186).

2 eggplant, cut into ¼-inch-thick slices

Spread the eggplant slices on the dehydrator tray. Dry until leathery and no moisture remains.

OVEN	DEHYDRATOR
125°F, 10 to 12 hours	125°F, 8 to 10 hours

PER SERVING (¼ CUP) CALORIES: 35; FAT: 0G; CARBS: 8G; SUGAR: 4G; FIBER: 4G; PROTEIN: 2G; SODIUM: 4MG

Garlic

YIELD ½ cup ❖ PREP TIME 10 minutes ❖ PRETREATMENT roasting (optional)

Dried garlic makes a delicious garlic powder, but to really amp up the flavor, first roast the garlic in the oven. Simply slice the top off a whole head of garlic to reveal the cloves. Place it in a square of parchment paper or aluminum foil, drizzle with a teaspoon of olive oil, close the parchment into a neat package, and roast for 45 minutes at 350°F. When cool, remove the cloves and dehydrate per the recipe instructions.

4 heads garlic

1. Remove the cloves from the head of garlic and discard their papery skins.

2. Spread the garlic cloves on the dehydrator trays. Dry until shriveled and crisp.

OVEN	DEHYDRATOR
125°F, 10 to 12 hours	125°F, 8 to 10 hours

PER SERVING (1 TSP) CALORIES: 17; FAT: 0G; CARBS: 4G; SUGAR: 0G; FIBER: 0G; PROTEIN: 1G; SODIUM: 2MG

Ginger

YIELD ¼ cup ❖ PREP TIME 10 minutes ❖ PRETREATMENT none

My absolute favorite application for dried ginger is in holiday baked goods, especially pumpkin pie and Pumpkin Bread (page 156). A slice of dried ginger can also be added to hot water to make a tummy-soothing tea.

1 (8-inch) knob fresh ginger, peeled

1. Cut the ginger into ⅛-inch-thick slices.
2. Spread the slices on the dehydrator trays. Dry until shriveled and crisp.

OVEN	DEHYDRATOR
125°F, 6 to 10 hours	125°F, 4 to 8 hours

PER SERVING (1 TSP) CALORIES: 8; FAT: 0G; CARBS: 2G; SUGAR: 0G; FIBER: 0G; PROTEIN: 0G; SODIUM: 0MG

Green Beans

YIELD 1 to 2 cups ✳ PREP TIME 10 minutes ✳ PRETREATMENT blanch

Dried green beans are delicious when added to Minestrone Soup (page 176) or stirred into casseroles. They can also be rehydrated in hot water and served as a side dish.

Sea salt

1 pound green beans, stems and strings removed and discarded, cut into 1-inch pieces

1. Prepare an ice-water bath and set aside. Bring a large saucepan of salted water to a boil.

2. Cook the green beans for 3 minutes. Drain and plunge into the ice water. Drain and pat dry with paper towels.

3. Spread the green beans on the dehydrator tray lined with a silicone mat. Dry until brittle.

OVEN	DEHYDRATOR
125°F, 8 to 10 hours	125°F, 6 to 8 hours

PER SERVING (¼ CUP) CALORIES: 18; FAT: 0G; CARBS: 4G; SUGAR: 1G; FIBER: 2G; PROTEIN: 1G; SODIUM: 19MG

Herbs: Botanical

YIELD varies ❋ PREP TIME 5 minutes ❋ PRETREATMENT none

Botanical herbs are more delicate than perennial herbs and are typically added at the end of cooking. They include a wide array of biennial and annual plants, including basil, mint, tarragon, chives, dill, and cilantro. Unlike perennial herbs, the stems of these tender herbs can be eaten and often contain more flavor than the leaves (though I generally discard mint stems). As a general rule, 6 herb sprigs yield about 1 tablespoon of dried herb.

1 bunch fresh herbs, such as basil, tarragon, chives, or dill,
   rinsed and patted or spun dry

1. Separate the leaves of the herbs so they do not clump together. Do not remove them from the stems.

2. Spread the herbs on the dehydrator trays. Dry just until crisp. Remove the leaves from the stems, if desired, but do not crumble until ready to use.

OVEN	DEHYDRATOR
105°F, 4 to 6 hours	105°F, 3 to 4 hours

Herbs: Perennial

YIELD varies ✵ PREP TIME 5 minutes ✵ PRETREATMENT none

Perennial herbs have woody stems and include thyme, rosemary, bay, and lavender. These herbs are often used in savory cooking and can be added early in the cooking process to infuse dishes with flavor. Dried perennial herbs can be combined with dried botanical herbs (page 85) for blends such as Herbes de Provence (page 88) and Italian Herb Blend (page 88).

12 sprigs fresh herbs, such as rosemary or thyme, rinsed and patted, or spun dry

1. Leave the leaves on the woody stems while dehydrating.
2. Spread the sprigs on the dehydrator trays. Dry just until crisp. When cool, remove the leaves from the stems. Do not crush until ready to use.

OVEN	DEHYDRATOR
115°F, 6 to 8 hours	115°F, 4 to 6 hours

COOKING WITH HERBS

Let the aromatic combinations of these two traditional herb blends transport your dishes to lush European countryside kitchens.

HERBES DE PROVENCE YIELD 1 cup

Experience the flavors of France. Lavender is not traditional in this seasoning, but it adds a beautiful aroma. Use the drying techniques for both Herbs: Botanical (page 85) and Herbs: Perennial (page 87) to make this blend.

3 tablespoons dried thyme

2 tablespoons dried rosemary

2 tablespoons dried basil

2 tablespoons dried marjoram

2 tablespoons dried savory

1 teaspoon dried lavender flowers (optional)

1 teaspoon dried oregano

After drying, mix the thyme, rosemary, basil, marjoram, savory, lavender flowers (if using), and oregano. Store in an airtight container.

ITALIAN HERB BLEND YIELD 1 cup

While Italian seasonings are widely available in your grocery store, imagine the delicious aromas wafting from your kitchen when you use your own authentic, almost-like-fresh, salt-free Italian herb blend. Enhance your marinara, ratatouille, lasagna, or any savory tomato-based dishes with this blend. Use the drying techniques for both Herbs: Botanical (page 85) and Herbs: Perennial (page 87) to make this blend.

¼ cup dried oregano

¼ cup dried basil

¼ cup dried thyme

2 tablespoons dried marjoram

2 tablespoons dried rosemary leaves

After drying, mix the oregano, basil, thyme, marjoram, and rosemary leaves. Store in an airtight container.

Kale & Other Leafy Greens

YIELD 2 cups ❖ PREP TIME 5 minutes ❖ PRETREATMENT none

Kale chips may not be as ubiquitous as they once were, but they're still a delicious vegan source of protein, fiber, vitamins, and minerals. Dried kale is also awesome when ground into a fine powder and added to smoothies, such as the Power Greens Smoothie (page 152). Choose any variety of kale that you enjoy. I like Lacinato for drying because it has thick leaves and lies relatively flat. Curly leaf varieties also offer a nice texture when dried. This method also works for other leafy greens, such as spinach and chard, though drying times will vary.

1 bunch kale, thoroughly washed and dried

1. Remove the tough ribs from the kale leaves and save for another use. Keep the leaves whole or tear into bite-size pieces.

2. Spread the kale on the dehydrator trays. Dry until crisp.

OVEN	DEHYDRATOR
115°F, 4 to 8 hours	115°F, 3 to 6 hours

PER SERVING (¼ CUP) CALORIES: 25; FAT: 0G; CARBS: 5G; SUGAR: 0G; FIBER: 1G; PROTEIN: 2G; SODIUM: 22MG

Leeks

YIELD 1 to 2 cups ❖ PREP TIME 10 minutes ❖ PRETREATMENT none

Leeks are part of the onion family and are used often in fine cooking, particularly French cuisine. Dried leeks add a depth of flavor to broth and can be added to nearly any savory dish for flavor and complexity.

4 leeks, white and pale green parts only, roots removed

1. Halve the leeks lengthwise, and cut into ¼-inch-thick slices. Rinse thoroughly under cool running water. Squeeze out the excess moisture and then blot dry with paper towels.

2. Spread the leeks on the dehydrator trays lined with silicone mats or screens. Dry until crisp and airy.

OVEN	DEHYDRATOR
125°F, 8 to 10 hours	125°F, 6 to 8 hours

PER SERVING (¼ CUP) CALORIES: 54; FAT: 0G; CARBS: 13G; SUGAR: 4G; FIBER: 2G; PROTEIN: 1G; SODIUM: 18MG

Mushrooms

YIELD 2 to 4 cups ❖ PREP TIME 5 minutes ❖ PRETREATMENT none

Dried mushrooms can be rehydrated and added to a wide variety of savory dishes. My favorite use is to grind dried mushrooms to a fine powder and use as a coating for meat or in Mushroom & Pea Risotto (page 188). You can use any variety of mushroom here; just make sure to clean away any dirt and ensure the pieces are uniform and small. If you want to dry a large, whole portobello mushroom, cut it into slices or it will take a very long time to dry.

1 pound mushrooms

1. Rinse the mushrooms in cold water and dry them thoroughly with paper towels.

2. Cut dense mushrooms, such as portobello, cremini, or button, into ½-inch-thick slices. Halve oyster, shiitake, and maitake mushrooms, or keep whole.

3. Spread the mushrooms on the dehydrator trays. Dry until no moisture remains. Some mushrooms become crisp and lightweight when dried while others curl and become leathery.

OVEN	DEHYDRATOR
125°F, 6 to 8 hours	125°F, 4 to 6 hours

PER SERVING (¼ CUP) CALORIES: 12; FAT: 0G; CARBS: 2G; SUGAR: 1G; FIBER: 1G; PROTEIN: 2G; SODIUM: 3MG

Onions

YIELD 2 cups ✣ PREP TIME 10 minutes ✣ PRETREATMENT none

Dried onions let you get one good cry out during preparation and then you're set for several future meals. Add dried onions to dried celery and carrots for a mirepoix, which serves as a flavoring agent. Dried onions can also be ground to a fine powder and added to an endless array of savory foods.

4 whole onions, peeled and cut into ¼-inch dice

Spread the onions on the dehydrator trays lined with silicone mats or screens. Dry until crisp and shrunk.

OVEN	DEHYDRATOR
125°F, 10 to 12 hours	125°F, 8 to 10 hours

PER SERVING (¼ CUP) CALORIES: 22; FAT: 0G; CARBS: 5G; SUGAR: 2G; FIBER: 1G; PROTEIN: 1G; SODIUM: 2MG

Peas

YIELD 1 cup ✣ PREP TIME 10 minutes ✣ PRETREATMENT blanch

Dehydrated peas are so versatile. They can be added to soups and casseroles or rehydrated and served as a hot side dish or used cold, tossed in salads. They're also delicious in Mushroom & Pea Risotto (page 188). When drying, you can use frozen, defrosted peas and skip the pretreatment.

Sea salt   2 cups fresh, shelled peas

1. Prepare an ice-water bath and set aside. Bring a medium saucepan of salted water to a boil.

2. Cook the peas for 2 minutes. Drain and plunge into the ice water. Drain and pat dry with paper towels.

3. Spread the peas on the dehydrator tray lined with a silicone mat or screen. Dry until brittle.

OVEN	DEHYDRATOR
125°F, 6 to 8 hours	125°F, 4 to 6 hours

PER SERVING (¼ CUP) CALORIES: 59; FAT: 0G; CARBS: 11G; SUGAR: 4G; FIBER: 4G; PROTEIN: 4G; SODIUM: 35MG

Peppers

YIELD varies ❋ PREP TIME 10 minutes ❋ PRETREATMENT charring (optional)

Whether you choose mild bell peppers or hot varieties, such as serrano or jalapeño, dried peppers are a versatile pantry staple. Prepare the peppers based on how you intend to use them. For example, hot peppers usually are ground into a powder to add to cooking, whereas bell peppers may be left in strips or diced to add to savory dishes. For added flavor, cook peppers over an open flame or under the broiler until charred, place in a covered container for 10 minutes, and then peel, stem, and seed before slicing.

4 bell peppers or 24 hot peppers, rinsed, patted dry, halved, stemmed, and seeded

1. Cut the bell peppers into long strips or ¼-inch dice. Hot peppers may be dried whole, but will require a much longer drying time. If you prefer more heat with your hot peppers, leave the stems, seeds, and membranes intact.

2. Spread the peppers on the dehydrator trays lined with silicone mats or screens for smaller pieces. Dry until shrunk and brittle.

OVEN	DEHYDRATOR
135°F, 10 to 12 hours	125°F, 8 to 10 hours

PER SERVING (¼ CUP) CALORIES: 18; FAT: 0G; CARBS: 4G; SUGAR: 3G; FIBER: 1G; PROTEIN: 1G; SODIUM: 2MG

Potatoes

YIELD 4 cups ❊ PREP TIME 10 minutes ❊ PRETREATMENT lemon juice, blanch

Dried potatoes can be used for many purposes—from breakfast hash to soups to back-packing meals. If you plan to cook them with moist heat, such as in a soup or casserole, no rehydrating is necessary. If you plan to cook with a dry heat, such as panfrying, soak overnight in cold water and drain thoroughly before adding to a skillet.

¼ cup freshly squeezed lemon juice

Sea salt

2 pounds potatoes, peeled

1. Prepare an ice-water bath. Add the lemon juice to the bath and set aside. Bring a medium saucepan of salted water to a boil.

2. Cut the potatoes into ⅛-inch-thick rounds, ¼-inch dice, or shred using a food processor or box grater. Cook for 5 minutes. Drain and plunge into the lemon–ice water. Drain and pat dry with paper towels.

3. Spread the potatoes on the dehydrator tray lined with a silicone mat. Dry until brittle and no moisture remains.

OVEN	DEHYDRATOR
125°F, 10 to 12 hours	125°F, 8 to 10 hours

PER SERVING (¼ CUP) CALORIES: 40; FAT: 0G; CARBS: 9G; SUGAR: 1G; FIBER: 1G; PROTEIN: 1G; SODIUM: 12MG

Root Vegetables

YIELD 2 cups ❁ PREP TIME 10 minutes ❁ PRETREATMENT blanch

Root vegetables, such as parsnips, sweet potatoes, carrots, and turnips, are great for drying and can be rehydrated to add to savory recipes. Root vegetables also make delicious chips when sliced very thinly. Simply blanch for an extra 3 to 5 minutes, until tender, before drying.

Sea salt   2 pounds root vegetables, peeled

1. Prepare an ice-water bath and set aside. Bring a large saucepan of salted water to a boil.

2. Cut the vegetables into $\frac{1}{2}$-inch dice. Cook for 5 to 6 minutes. Drain and plunge into the ice water. Drain and pat dry with paper towels.

3. Spread the vegetables on the dehydrator tray lined with a silicone mat. Dry until brittle.

OVEN	DEHYDRATOR
125°F, 10 to 12 hours	125°F, 8 to 10 hours

PER SERVING (¼ CUP) CALORIES: 85; FAT: 0G; CARBS: 20G; SUGAR: 5G; FIBER: 6G; PROTEIN: 1G; SODIUM: 27MG

Squash

YIELD 4 cups ❄ PREP TIME 10 minutes ❄ PRETREATMENT blanch

I love winter squashes. The applications for squash are endless, but my family's favorite is in quick bread. Rich grew up enjoying Pumpkin Bread (page 156). Other nontraditional squashes, such as kabocha, make an excellent addition to sweet dishes. Squash is also awesome rehydrated for casseroles.

Sea salt

1 (2- to 3-pound) squash, such as butternut, kabocha, or pumpkin, halved, seeds and strings removed

1. Prepare an ice-water bath and set aside. Bring a medium saucepan of salted water to a boil.
2. Carefully cut away the skin from the squash halves. Cut the flesh into 1-inch pieces. Cook for 5 minutes. Drain and plunge into the ice water. Drain and pat dry with paper towels.
3. Spread the squash on the dehydrator tray. Dry until shrunk, hard, and no moisture remains.

OVEN	DEHYDRATOR
125°F, 12 to 14 hours	125°F, 10 to 12 hours

PER SERVING (¼ CUP) CALORIES: 24; FAT: 0G; CARBS: 6G; SUGAR: 1G; FIBER: 1G; PROTEIN: 1G; SODIUM: 10MG

Tomatoes

YIELD 2 cups ❖ PREP TIME 10 minutes ❖ PRETREATMENT none

You probably already know that tomatoes are a fruit, but you'll discover just how sweet they can be when you dehydrate them. I couldn't stop snacking on the first batch of dried tomatoes I made and never got around to storing them, much less using them in any recipes. They are that good! It should go without saying that they far surpass conventional packaged sun-dried tomatoes. They're delicious in Minestrone Soup (page 176) and Cream of Tomato Soup (page 169) or simply eaten as a snack.

2 pounds small vine-ripened tomatoes, rinsed and patted dry

1. Halve the tomatoes and remove the seeds and pulp with your fingers.
2. Place the tomatoes skin-side down on the dehydrator trays. Dry until leathery and beginning to crisp around the edges.

OVEN	DEHYDRATOR
125°F, 12 to 14 hours	125°F, 8 to 12 hours

PER SERVING (¼ CUP) CALORIES: 20; FAT: 0G; CARBS: 4G; SUGAR: 3G; FIBER: 1G; PROTEIN: 1G; SODIUM: 6MG

Zucchini

YIELD 2 cups ❖ PREP TIME 10 minutes ❖ PRETREATMENT none

Zucchini and other summer squash are another delicious vegetable to dehydrate and eat as a snack or use as a chip. They can also be roughly ground to make a coating for meat or fish, or diced and used in soups or pasta dishes.

4 zucchini, rinsed and patted dry

1. Slice the unpeeled zucchini into paper-thin slices to make chips, shred or cut into matchsticks, or cut into ¼-inch dice.
2. Spread the zucchini on the dehydrator trays. Dry until crisp and translucent. Pieces should be shrunken, brittle, and free from moisture.

OVEN	DEHYDRATOR
125°F, 10 to 12 hours	125°F, 8 to 10 hours

PER SERVING (¼ CUP) CALORIES: 16; FAT: 0G; CARBS: 3G; SUGAR: 2G; FIBER: 1G; PROTEIN: 1G; SODIUM: 10MG

PART THREE

DEHYDRATED FOOD RECIPES

CHAPTER SIX
Dried Meats & Jerkies

CHAPTER SEVEN
Snacks

CHAPTER EIGHT
Raw Foods

Dried Meats & Jerkies

Classic Beef Jerky 104

Teriyaki Beef Jerky 105

Ground Beef Jerky 106

Spicy Ground Beef
Jerky 107

Basic Chicken
Jerky 108

Ginger-Soy Chicken
Jerky 109

Duck Jerky 110

Basic Venison Jerky 111

Teriyaki Venison
Jerky 112

Fish Jerky 113

Classic Beef Jerky

YIELD 4 ounces ❊ PREP TIME 20 minutes, plus 1 hour inactive time
COOK TIME 10 to 15 minutes ❊ DRY TIME 6 to 8 hours

This recipe offers traditional jerky flavor but much less sodium and sugar than you'll find in commercial varieties. Precooking meat to an internal temperature of 160° to 165°F eliminates pathogenic bacteria, including E. coli. The USDA says precooking is the safest method for making jerky, versus finishing it in the oven or skipping the step altogether.

1 pound beef steak, trimmed of all visible fat

2 tablespoons low-sodium soy sauce

2 tablespoons Worcestershire sauce

1 teaspoon maple syrup

1 tablespoon puréed onion (see Tip)

1 teaspoon puréed fresh garlic (see Tip)

1 teaspoon smoked paprika

¼ teaspoon cayenne pepper

Freshly ground black pepper

1. Freeze the beef for about 20 minutes to firm it up, which makes slicing it easier.

2. In a small bowl, whisk the soy sauce, Worcestershire sauce, maple syrup, onion, garlic, paprika, and cayenne pepper. Season with black pepper. Set aside.

3. Thinly slice the beef across the grain. Place the slices in a shallow nonreactive dish and pour the soy sauce mixture over. Refrigerate for at least 1 hour, or up to overnight.

4. Preheat the oven to 325°F. Preheat the dehydrator and the dehydrator tray to between 145° and 155°F.

5. Shake the excess liquid from the beef slices. Place them on a rack in a rimmed baking sheet. Bake for 10 to 15 minutes, depending on the thickness of the meat, until cooked through (to an internal temperature of 160°F).

6. Immediately transfer the cooked beef slices to the preheated dehydrator tray. Dry for 6 to 8 hours, until leathery but not crisp.

PREPARATION TIP: Use a Microplane grater to purée the onion and garlic, which will spread evenly throughout the marinade.

PER SERVING (½ OUNCE) CALORIES: 114; FAT: 4G; CARBS: 2G; SUGAR: 2G; FIBER: 0G; PROTEIN: 18G; SODIUM: 299MG

Teriyaki Beef Jerky

YIELD 4 ounces ❋ PREP TIME 20 minutes, plus 1 hour inactive time
COOK TIME 10 to 15 minutes ❋ DRY TIME 6 to 8 hours

You could certainly buy teriyaki sauce to make this recipe, but I prefer to make my own and avoid unnatural food additives, preservatives, and excess sugar present in commercial varieties. Plus, I love saving money by doing it myself.

1 pound beef steak, trimmed of all
   visible fat

¼ cup low-sodium soy sauce

2 tablespoons maple syrup
   or brown sugar

1 tablespoon rice wine vinegar

1 teaspoon puréed garlic
   (see Tip, page 104)

1 teaspoon puréed ginger
   (see Tip, page 104)

¼ teaspoon cayenne pepper

1. Freeze the beef for about 20 minutes to firm it up, which makes slicing it easier.

2. In a small bowl, whisk the soy sauce, maple syrup, vinegar, garlic, ginger, and cayenne pepper. Set aside.

3. Thinly slice the beef across the grain. Place the slices in a shallow nonreactive dish and cover with the teriyaki sauce mixture. Refrigerate for at least 1 hour or up to overnight.

4. Preheat the oven to 325°F. Preheat the dehydrator and the dehydrator tray to between 145° and 155°F.

5. Shake the excess liquid from the beef slices. Place them on a rack in a rimmed baking sheet. Bake for 10 to 15 minutes, depending on the thickness of the meat, until cooked through (to an internal temperature of 160°F).

6. Immediately transfer the cooked beef slices to the dehydrator tray. Dry for 6 to 8 hours, or until leathery but not crisp.

NUTRITIONAL HIGHLIGHT: Use a gluten-free soy sauce if you are sensitive to wheat or are gluten-intolerant.

PER SERVING (½ OUNCE) CALORIES: 123; FAT: 4G; CARBS: 4G; SUGAR: 4G; FIBER: 0G; PROTEIN: 18G; SODIUM: 481MG

Ground Beef Jerky

YIELD 8 ounces ✳ PREP TIME 15 minutes ✳ COOK TIME 10 to 15 minutes
DRY TIME 8 to 10 hours

When using ground meat, it is even more important to bake it to an internal temperature of 160°F before dehydrating in order to minimize the risk of foodborne toxins. This recipe has mellow flavors for a kid-friendly snack.

2 pounds ground beef, 85 percent lean

1 tablespoon Worcestershire sauce

1 teaspoon low-sodium soy sauce

1 tablespoon sea salt

1 teaspoon freshly ground black pepper

1 teaspoon onion powder

½ teaspoon garlic powder

1. Preheat the oven to 350°F. Preheat the dehydrator and the dehydrator tray to 155°F.

2. Line a baking sheet with parchment paper.

3. In a medium bowl, thoroughly mix the ground beef, Worcestershire sauce, soy sauce, salt, pepper, onion powder, and garlic powder with your clean hands.

4. Place the beef mixture in a jerky gun or use a cake-decorating bag fitted with a ½-inch plain tip. Pipe the beef onto the prepared baking sheet in long, narrow strips.

5. Bake for 10 to 15 minutes, until the meat is cooked through (to an internal temperature of 160°F).

6. Transfer the parchment paper to the dehydrator trays. Dehydrate for 4 hours. Turn the jerky over and dehydrate for 4 to 6 hours more, or until tender and chewy but thoroughly dry.

PREPARATION TIP: Use two sheets of parchment paper on the baking sheet and pipe the meat onto the pan widthwise instead of lengthwise. This allows you to divide the parchment evenly between two dehydrator trays after baking.

PER SERVING (½ OUNCE) CALORIES: 108; FAT: 4G; CARBS: 1G; SUGAR: 0G; FIBER: 0G; PROTEIN: 17G; SODIUM: 417MG

Spicy Ground Beef Jerky

YIELD 8 ounces ❖ PREP TIME 15 minutes ❖ COOK TIME 10 to 15 minutes
DRY TIME 8 to 10 hours

Spice things up with this healthy take on the convenience store staple. If you cannot find chipotle powder, simply omit it or use ½ teaspoon of smoked paprika.

2 pounds ground beef, 85 percent lean

1½ tablespoons Worcestershire sauce

1 tablespoon sea salt

1 teaspoon freshly ground black pepper

1 teaspoon chipotle powder

1 teaspoon onion powder

1 teaspoon garlic powder

½ teaspoon cayenne pepper

1. Preheat your oven to 350°F. Preheat the dehydrator and the dehydrator tray to 155°F.

2. Line a baking sheet with parchment paper.

3. In a medium bowl, thoroughly mix the ground beef, Worcestershire sauce, salt, black pepper, chipotle powder, onion powder, garlic powder, and cayenne pepper thoroughly with clean hands.

4. Place the beef mixture in a jerky gun or use a cake-decorating bag fitted with a ½-inch plain tip. Pipe the beef mixture onto the prepared baking sheet in long, narrow strips.

5. Bake for 10 to 15 minutes, until cooked through (to an internal temperature of 160°F).

6. Transfer the parchment paper to the dehydrator trays. Dehydrate for 4 hours. Turn over the jerky and dehydrate for 4 to 6 hours more, or until tender and chewy but thoroughly dry.

PER SERVING (½ OUNCE) CALORIES: 108; FAT: 4G; CARBS: 1G; SUGAR: 0G; FIBER: 0G; PROTEIN: 17G; SODIUM: 404MG

Basic Chicken Jerky

YIELD 4 to 6 ounces ❄ PREP TIME 20 minutes, plus 30 minutes to 1 hour inactive time
COOK TIME 10 to 15 minutes ❄ DRY TIME 6 to 8 hours

Chicken is naturally low in fat, making it a great meat for drying. It's also a good source of protein. This recipe makes great snacks for the trail or anytime you're not close to a kitchen but need good-quality sustenance.

2 (8-ounce) boneless skinless chicken breasts, trimmed of all visible fat

1 tablespoon apple cider vinegar

1 tablespoon maple syrup or brown sugar

¼ teaspoon sea salt

¼ teaspoon cayenne pepper

1. Freeze the chicken for about 20 minutes to firm it up, which makes slicing it easier.

2. In a small bowl, whisk together the vinegar, maple syrup, sea salt, and cayenne pepper. Set aside.

3. Thinly slice the chicken across the grain, about ⅛ inch thick. Place the slices in a shallow nonreactive dish and cover with the sauce. Refrigerate for 30 minutes to 1 hour.

4. Preheat the oven to 325°F. Preheat the dehydrator and the dehydrator tray to between 145° and 155°F.

5. Place the chicken slices on an ovenproof rack in a rimmed baking sheet. Bake for 10 to 15 minutes, depending on the thickness of the meat, until cooked through (to an internal temperature of 165°F).

6. Immediately transfer the cooked chicken to the dehydrator tray. Dry for 6 to 8 hours, or until leathery but not crisp.

NUTRITIONAL HIGHLIGHT: Maple syrup, while easier to whisk into the marinade, contains the same amount of sugar as the brown sugar so it is not necessarily a healthier choice.

PER SERVING (½ OUNCE) CALORIES: 115; FAT: 4G; CARBS: 2G; SUGAR: 2G; FIBER: 0G; PROTEIN: 16G; SODIUM: 150MG

Ginger-Soy Chicken Jerky

YIELD 4 to 6 ounces ❖ PREP TIME 20 minutes, plus 30 minutes to 1 hour inactive time
COOK TIME 10 to 15 minutes ❖ DRY TIME 6 to 8 hours

Ginger, garlic, and soy sauce are classic Asian flavors and make this chicken jerky an addictive snack. Decrease the cayenne if you're making this jerky for children or prefer a milder spice.

2 (8-ounce) boneless, skinless chicken breasts, trimmed of all visible fat

¼ cup low-sodium soy sauce

1 tablespoon freshly squeezed lime juice

1 teaspoon puréed fresh ginger (See Tip)

1 teaspoon puréed garlic (See Tip)

¼ teaspoon cayenne pepper

1. Freeze the chicken for about 20 minutes to firm it up, which makes slicing it easier.

2. In a small bowl, whisk the soy sauce, lime juice, ginger, garlic, and cayenne pepper.

3. Thinly slice the chicken across the grain, about ⅛ inch thick. Place the slices in a shallow nonreactive dish and cover with the sauce. Refrigerate for 30 minutes to 1 hour.

4. Preheat the oven to 325°F. Preheat the dehydrator and the dehydrator tray to between 145° and 155°F.

5. Place the chicken slices on an ovenproof rack in a rimmed baking sheet. Bake for 10 to 15 minutes, depending on the thickness of the meat, until cooked through (to an internal temperature of 165°F).

6. Immediately transfer the cooked chicken to the dehydrator tray. Dry for 6 to 8 hours, or until leathery but not crisp.

PREPARATION TIP: Use a Microplane grater to purée the onion and garlic, which will spread evenly throughout the marinade.

PER SERVING (½ OUNCE) CALORIES: 112; FAT: 4G; CARBS: 1G; SUGAR: 1G; FIBER: 0G; PROTEIN: 17G; SODIUM: 487MG

Duck Jerky

YIELD 4 ounces ✻ PREP TIME 20 minutes, plus 2 hours inactive time
COOK TIME 10 to 15 minutes ✻ DRY TIME 6 to 8 hours

Duck is my favorite variety of poultry. It is naturally rich in minerals, giving it a beautiful complexity of flavor. Make sure to trim the meat of any skin and fat before dehydrating it. Fat contributes to rapid spoilage.

1 pound duck breast, skin and
    fat removed

¼ cup low-sodium soy sauce

¼ cup water

1 teaspoon maple syrup or brown sugar

1 teaspoon minced fresh thyme

1 teaspoon sea salt

Freshly ground black pepper

1. Freeze the duck for about 20 minutes to firm it up, which makes slicing it easier.

2. In a small bowl, whisk the soy sauce, water, maple syrup, thyme, salt, and a few grinds of black pepper.

3. Thinly slice the duck across the grain, about ⅛ inch thick. Place the slices in a shallow nonreactive dish and cover with the sauce. Refrigerate for at least 2 hours or up to 24 hours.

4. Preheat the oven to 325°F. Preheat the dehydrator and the dehydrator tray to between 145° and 155°F.

5. Shake off the excess moisture on the duck slices. Place them on an ovenproof rack in a rimmed baking sheet. Bake for 10 to 15 minutes, depending on the thickness of the meat, until cooked through (to an internal temperature of 165°F).

6. Immediately transfer the cooked duck to the dehydrator tray. Dry for 6 to 8 hours, or until leathery but not crisp.

COOKING TIP: Don't toss that duck fat. Cut it into 2-inch pieces and simmer it over low heat with about ⅛ cup of water for 45 minutes to 1 hour, until the fat is rendered and the water has evaporated. Cool slightly, strain into a heatproof container, and refrigerate. It makes a delicious fat for cooking vegetables or making duck confit.

PER SERVING (½ OUNCE) CALORIES: 78; FAT: 2G; CARBS: 1G; SUGAR: 1G; FIBER: 0G; PROTEIN: 13G; SODIUM: 674MG

Basic Venison Jerky

YIELD 8 to 12 ounces ❋ PREP TIME 20 minutes, plus 3 hours inactive time
COOK TIME 10 to 15 minutes ❋ DRY TIME 6 to 8 hours

If you are lucky enough to find yourself with fresh venison, you probably have more meat on your hands than you can use immediately. Making jerky is one of the most economical and flavorful methods for storing the excess meat. As with other meats but especially with wild game, cooking venison beforehand is essential for food safety.

2 pounds venison meat, trimmed
   of all visible fat

½ cup low-sodium soy sauce

½ cup Worcestershire sauce

1 tablespoon maple syrup

1 teaspoon smoked paprika

¼ teaspoon cayenne pepper

1. Freeze the venison for about 20 minutes to firm it up, which makes slicing it easier.

2. In a small bowl, whisk the soy sauce, Worcestershire sauce, maple syrup, paprika, and cayenne pepper.

3. Thinly slice the venison against the grain, ⅛ to ¼ inch thick. Put the slices in a shallow nonreactive dish and cover with the sauce. Refrigerate for at least 3 hours, or up to 6 hours.

4. Preheat the oven to 325°F. Preheat the dehydrator and dehydrator tray to between 145° and 155°F.

5. Shake the excess liquid from the venison slices. Place them on an ovenproof rack in a rimmed baking sheet. Bake for 10 to 15 minutes, depending on the thickness of the meat, until cooked through (to a minimum internal temperature of 145°F).

6. Immediately transfer the cooked venison to the dehydrator tray. Dry for 6 to 8 hours, or until leathery but not crisp.

NUTRITIONAL HIGHLIGHT: Venison is rich in iron, naturally low in fat, and high in protein.

PER SERVING (½ OUNCE) CALORIES: 75; FAT: 1G; CARBS: 3G; SUGAR: 3G; FIBER: 0G; PROTEIN: 13G; SODIUM: 523MG

Teriyaki Venison Jerky

YIELD 8 to 12 ounces ❋ PREP TIME 20 minutes, plus 3 hours inactive time
COOK TIME 10 to 15 minutes ❋ DRY TIME 6 to 8 hours

This recipe has the perfect balance of salty, sour, and sweet. Try not to eat it all in one sitting!

2 pounds venison meat, trimmed
of all visible fat

½ cup low-sodium soy sauce

¼ cup rice wine vinegar

2 tablespoons honey or brown sugar

1 tablespoon minced peeled fresh ginger

1 teaspoon onion powder

¼ teaspoon cayenne pepper

1. Freeze the venison for about 20 minutes to firm it up, which makes slicing it easier.

2. In a small bowl, whisk the soy sauce, vinegar, honey, ginger, onion powder, and cayenne pepper.

3. Thinly slice the venison against the grain, $\frac{1}{8}$ to $\frac{1}{4}$ inch thick. Place the slices in a shallow nonreactive dish and cover with the teriyaki sauce mixture. Refrigerate for at least 3 hours, or up to 6 hours.

4. Preheat the oven to 325°F. Preheat the dehydrator and dehydrator tray to between 145° and 155°F.

5. Shake the excess liquid from the venison slices. Place on an ovenproof rack in a rimmed baking sheet. Bake for 10 to 15 minutes, depending on the thickness of the meat, until cooked through (to a minimum internal temperature of 145°F).

6. Immediately transfer the cooked venison to the dehydrator tray. Dry for 6 to 8 hours, or until leathery but not crisp.

PER SERVING (½ OUNCE) CALORIES: 76; FAT: 1G; CARBS: 3G; SUGAR: 3G; FIBER: 0G; PROTEIN: 13G; SODIUM: 440MG

Fish Jerky

YIELD 4 ounces ✽ PREP TIME 20 minutes, plus 2 hours inactive time
COOK TIME 0 minutes ✽ DRY TIME 4 to 6 hours

Fish jerky is surprisingly delicious. This version has a sweet and tangy tropical kick.

1 pound fresh, lean, firm fish fillets, such as bass, tuna, or snapper, skin removed, trimmed of all visible fat

¼ cup pineapple juice (from canned pineapple; see Tip)

¼ cup low-sodium soy sauce

1 teaspoon puréed garlic (See Tip, page 109)

1 teaspoon puréed ginger (See Tip, page 109)

Freshly ground black pepper

1. Freeze the fish for about 20 minutes to firm it up, which makes slicing it easier.

2. In a small bowl, whisk the pineapple juice, soy sauce, garlic, ginger, and a few grinds of pepper.

3. Thinly slice the fish across the grain, $\frac{1}{8}$ to $\frac{1}{4}$ inch thick. Put in a shallow nonreactive dish and cover with the sauce. Refrigerate for at least 2 hours, or up to 4 hours.

4. Preheat the dehydrator and dehydrator tray to between 145° and 155°F.

5. Shake the excess liquid from the fish slices. Place them on the dehydrator tray. Dry for 4 to 6 hours, or until leathery but not crisp.

INGREDIENT TIP: Do not use fresh pineapple juice. It contains enzymes that will break down the fish during the marinating time. Those enzymes are not present in cooked pineapple juice.

PER SERVING (½ OUNCE) CALORIES: 81; FAT: 1G; CARBS: 2G; SUGAR: 1G; FIBER: 0G; PROTEIN: 15G; SODIUM: 474MG

Snacks

Apple-Cinnamon Fruit Leather 116

Strawberry-Lime Fruit Leather 117

Ginger-Pear Fruit Leather 118

Pineapple Fruit Leather 119

Berry Lover's Trail Mix 120

Monkeying Around Trail Mix 121

Basic Energy Bars 122

Chocolate-Orange Energy Bars 123

Rosemary-Almond Crackers 124

Coconut Macaroons 125

Oatmeal Raisin Cookies 126

Salted Chocolate Chip Cookies 128

Pear Crisp 129

Apple-Cinnamon Fruit Leather

YIELD 8 fruit leathers ❋ PREP TIME 20 minutes ❋ COOK TIME 30 to 45 minutes
DRY TIME 8 to 12 hours

Apples and cinnamon are a classic flavor combination, especially in the fall when apples are falling from the trees faster than you can eat them. This recipe makes good use of the harvest and is a delicious apple treat you can enjoy long after the first frost. Fruit leathers are especially fun to include in kid's lunchboxes.

8 cups peeled, cored, diced apples

1 tablespoon ground cinnamon

1 tablespoon freshly squeezed lemon juice

1. Preheat the dehydrator to 135°F.

2. In small pot over medium-low heat, cook the apples for 20 to 30 minutes until slightly broken down. Use a potato masher to press them down gently as they cook. Remove from the heat.

3. With an immersion blender or in a countertop blender, purée the apples until smooth. Return the mixture to the heat. Stir in the cinnamon and lemon juice and cook for 10 to 15 minutes more.

4. Spread the mixture onto 2 to 3 dehydrator trays lined with silicone mats until it is about 1 inch from the edges. The thickness should be between $\frac{1}{8}$ and $\frac{1}{4}$ inch.

5. Dehydrate for 8 to 12 hours, rotating the trays 180 degrees about halfway through the drying time. The leather should peel easily off the mat. Cut into thin strips before rolling and storing in parchment paper.

PREPARATION TIP: You can line the silicone mat with parchment paper, if you wish, for easy packaging and storage.

PER SERVING (1 FRUIT LEATHER) CALORIES: 55; FAT: 0G; CARBS: 15G; SUGAR: 11G; FIBER: 2G; PROTEIN: 0G; SODIUM: 0MG

Strawberry-Lime Fruit Leather

YIELD 8 fruit leathers ❖ PREP TIME 5 minutes ❖ COOK TIME 0 minutes
DRY TIME 8 to 12 hours

The banana in this fruit leather adds a touch of sweetness. More important, it helps the fruit leather hold together and gives it structure. To keep the enzymes intact, you can dehydrate at a lower temperature. It takes slightly longer to dry but will remain raw if dried at less than 118°F.

8 cups hulled strawberries

1 ripe banana

Zest of 1 lime

Juice of 1 lime

1. Preheat the dehydrator to 135°F.

2. In a blender, purée the strawberries, banana, lime zest, and lime juice until smooth. Strain through a fine-mesh sieve to remove strawberry seeds, if you wish.

3. Spread the mixture on 2 to 3 dehydrator trays lined with silicone mats until about 1 inch from the edges. The thickness should be about ¼ inch, especially around the edges.

4. Dry for 8 to 12 hours, rotating the trays 180 degrees about halfway through the drying time. The leather should peel easily away from the silicone mat when finished drying. Cut into strips and wrap in parchment paper to store.

PER SERVING (1 FRUIT LEATHER) CALORIES: 51; FAT: 1G; CARBS: 14G; SUGAR: 9G; FIBER: 3G; PROTEIN: 1G; SODIUM: 2MG

Ginger-Pear Fruit Leather

YIELD 8 fruit leathers ❈ PREP TIME 10 minutes ❈ COOK TIME 15 to 20 minutes
DRY TIME 8 to 12 hours

I love the spicy flavor of ginger permeating this fruit leather. It has a slightly more grown-up flavor than other leathers. If you're serving it to children, you may want to reduce the amount of ginger.

8 cups peeled, cored, diced pears

1 teaspoon finely grated peeled
   fresh ginger

1 tablespoon freshly squeezed
   lemon juice

1. Preheat the dehydrator to 135°F.

2. In a large saucepan over medium-low heat, simmer the pears, ginger, and lemon juice for 15 to 20 minutes until broken down. Use a potato masher to press them down gently as they cook.

3. With an immersion blender or a countertop blender, purée the pears until smooth.

4. Pour the mixture onto 2 to 3 dehydrator trays lined with silicone mats until it is about 1 inch from the edges. The thickness should be about $\frac{1}{4}$ inch, especially around the edges.

5. Dry for 8 to 12 hours, rotating the trays 180 degrees about halfway through the drying time. The leather should peel easily away from the silicone mat when finished drying. Cut into thin strips and wrap in parchment paper to store.

PREPARATION TIP: Use a Microplane grater or a special tool for grating ginger to ensure it is puréed and has no chunks remaining.

PER SERVING (1 FRUIT LEATHER) CALORIES: 54; FAT: 0G; CARBS: 14G; SUGAR: 11G; FIBER: 2G;
PROTEIN: 0G; SODIUM: 0MG

Pineapple Fruit Leather

YIELD 8 leathers ❖ PREP TIME 5 minutes ❖ DRY TIME 8 to 12 hours

Pineapple is a rich source of enzymes. To keep them intact, dehydrate at a slightly lower temperature. For a flavorful spin on this treat, add one cup of fresh cilantro to the recipe. It turns the leather a pretty shade of green and gives it a delicious flavor complexity.

1 ripe pineapple, peeled, cored, and cut into chunks

1. Preheat the dehydrator to 125°F.

2. Purée the pineapple in a blender for 1 minute, or until very smooth.

3. Pour the mixture onto 2 to 3 dehydrator trays lined with silicone mats. Spread it out until it is about 1 inch from the edges. It should be about $\frac{1}{8}$ inch thick, and up to $\frac{1}{4}$ inch thick around the edges.

4. Dry for 8 to 12 hours, rotating the trays 180 degrees about halfway through the drying time, until no longer tacky and it peels easily from the silicone mat. Cut into thin strips and wrap in parchment paper to store.

NUTRITIONAL HIGHLIGHT: Pineapple contains the enzyme bromelain, which helps digest protein. Consider enjoying pineapple leather as a healthy dessert to aid in digestion.

PER SERVING (1 FRUIT LEATHER) CALORIES: 82; FAT: 0G; CARBS: 22G; SUGAR: 16G; FIBER: 2G; PROTEIN: 1G; SODIUM: 2MG

Berry Lover's Trail Mix

YIELD 4 cups ❊ PREP TIME 10 minutes, plus 6 hours inactive time
DRY TIME 6 to 8 hours

You could easily use the individual recipes listed in chapter 3 for making this trail mix. But, if you want to prepare it all at once, you need smaller portions of each ingredient, found here.

1 cup raw almonds

1 cup raw walnuts

1 cup raw cashews

Pinch of sea salt

2 cups fresh strawberries, washed, hulled, and quartered

2 cups fresh blueberries

1. In a large jar, combine the almonds, walnuts, and cashews with enough water to cover. Add the salt. Place the lid on the jar and soak for at least 6 hours or over-night. Rinse and drain thoroughly.

2. Preheat the dehydrator to 135°F.

3. Spread the nuts on 1 to 2 dehydrator trays.

4. Spread the strawberries on 2 dehydrator trays.

5. "Check" the blueberries by pressing the teeth of a serrated knife gently over the berries. Alternatively, blanch them in boiling water for 30 seconds, shock them in an ice-water bath, and pat dry with paper towels. Spread the blueberries over 1 to 2 dehydrator trays.

6. Dry the nuts, strawberries, and blueberries for 6 to 8 hours, or until the nuts are crunchy and the fruit is leathery. The nuts likely will be done before the fruit; remove the nut trays and set aside.

7. Mix the nuts and fruit together. Store in an airtight container.

PER SERVING (½ CUP) CALORIES: 296; FAT: 23G; CARBS: 18G; SUGAR: 7G; FIBER: 5G; PROTEIN: 9G; SODIUM: 35MG

Monkeying Around Trail Mix

YIELD 4 cups ❊ PREP TIME 10 minutes, plus 6 hours inactive time
DRY TIME 8 to 12 hours

Is there any better combination than chocolate, bananas, and nuts? My kids and I love it in smoothies, breakfast porridge, and, of course, trail mix.

2 cups raw almonds

1 cup raw cashews

Pinch of sea salt

6 ripe bananas

1 cup dark chocolate chips

1. In a large jar, combine the almonds and cashews with enough fresh water to cover. Add the salt. Place the lid on the jar and soak for at least 6 hours or overnight. Rinse and drain thoroughly.

2. Preheat the dehydrator to 135°F.

3. Spread the nuts on 1 to 2 dehydrator trays.

4. Cut the bananas into equal slices, $\frac{1}{8}$ to $\frac{1}{4}$ inch thick. Spread them on 1 to 2 dehydrator trays.

5. Dry the nuts and bananas for 8 to 12 hours, or until the nuts are crunchy and the fruit is leathery. The nuts likely will be done before the fruit; remove the trays and set aside.

6. Once completely cooled, mix the nuts, bananas, and chocolate. Store in an airtight container.

NUTRITIONAL HIGHLIGHT: Choose dark chocolate chips with at least 70 percent cacao for the greatest concentration of antioxidants and the least amount of sugar.

PER SERVING (½ CUP) CALORIES: 385; FAT: 24G; CARBS: 41G; SUGAR: 21G; FIBER: 6G; PROTEIN: 10G; SODIUM: 35MG

Basic Energy Bars

YIELD 6 to 8 bars ✳ PREP TIME 10 minutes, plus 6 hours inactive time
DRY TIME 8 to 10 hours

Dates are a natural source of sugar and sweeten these energy bars without the use of refined sugars or syrups. Use your favorite nuts instead of the almonds and walnuts, if you like. Macadamia nuts and shredded coconut are delicious in these bars. Simply keep the ratio between the dry ingredients and dates the same.

1 cup almonds

1 cup walnuts

Pinch of sea salt

1 cup pitted dates

1 cup shelled pepitas (pumpkin seeds) or shelled sunflower seeds

1 cup ground flaxseed

1 teaspoon vanilla extract

1. In a large jar, combine the almonds and walnuts with enough fresh water to cover. Add the salt. Place the lid on the jar and soak for 6 hours or overnight. Rinse and drain thoroughly.

2. Soak the dates in water for 30 minutes to soften. Drain thoroughly.

3. Preheat the dehydrator to 135°F.

4. Put the soaked nuts in a food processor and pulse until roughly chopped. Add the pepitas and flaxseed. Pulse once or twice just to incorporate.

5. In a medium bowl, purée the soaked dates with the vanilla using an immersion blender. Add to the nut mixture and blend just until incorporated.

6. Spread the mixture onto a dehydrator tray lined with a silicone mat, about $\frac{1}{2}$ inch thick. Slice into 4-inch-long rectangles.

7. Dry for 4 hours. When they're set and hold together easily, remove the bars from the silicone mat, flip, and place directly on the dehydrator tray. Dry for another 4 to 6 hours, or until set.

INGREDIENT TIP: *Save the soaking water from the dates to add to homemade almond milk as a natural sweetener.*

PER SERVING (1 BAR) CALORIES: 449; FAT: 30G; CARBS: 35G; SUGAR: 20G; FIBER: 12G; PROTEIN: 14G; SODIUM: 46MG

Chocolate-Orange Energy Bars

YIELD 6 to 8 bars ❖ PREP TIME 10 minutes, plus 6 hours inactive prep time
DRY TIME 8 to 10 hours

Chocolate and orange are a classic flavor combination. I love it in this deliciously sweet energy bar. Use good-quality cocoa powder for best results. My favorite is Equal Exchange Baking Cocoa.

2 cups pecans

Pinch of sea salt

1 cup pitted dates

Juice of 1 orange

Zest of 1 orange

1 teaspoon vanilla extract

1 cup ground flaxseed

¼ cup cocoa powder

1. In a large jar, combine the pecans with enough fresh water to cover. Add the salt. Place the lid on the jar and soak for 6 hours or overnight. Rinse and drain thoroughly.

2. Soak the dates in the orange juice, and enough water to cover, for 30 minutes to soften. Drain thoroughly, discarding the soaking liquid.

3. Preheat the dehydrator to 135°F.

4. In a medium bowl, purée the soaked dates with the vanilla and a generous pinch of sea salt, using an immersion blender.

5. Put the soaked nuts, flaxseed, and cocoa powder in a food processor and blend for 5 seconds.

6. Add the date purée. Blend just until incorporated.

7. Spread the mixture on a dehydrator tray lined with a silicone mat, about ½ inch thick. Slice into 4-inch-long rectangles.

8. Dry for 4 hours. When they're set and hold together easily, remove the bars from the silicone mat, flip, and place directly onto the dehydrator tray. Dry for another 4 to 6 hours, or until firm.

PER SERVING (1 BAR) CALORIES: 261; FAT: 13G; CARBS: 32G; SUGAR: 20G; FIBER: 10G; PROTEIN: 6G; SODIUM: 46MG

Rosemary-Almond Crackers

12 to 18 crackers ❖ PREP TIME 15 minutes ❖ DRY TIME 12 hours

I love enjoying Spanish tapas at home with good friends and a bottle of wine. Since I adopted a Paleo-style diet, I have wanted some form of grain-free cracker to slather with chicken liver pâté or roasted red pepper spread. This satisfies my cravings and even resembles the rosemary flatbread sold at gourmet markets.

1⅓ cups blanched almond flour

⅓ cup ground flaxseed

½ cup water

2 tablespoons extra-virgin olive oil

1 tablespoon minced fresh rosemary leaves

½ teaspoon sea salt

1. Preheat the dehydrator to 135°F.

2. In a food processor, pulse the almond flour, flaxseed, water, olive oil, rosemary, and sea salt until smooth.

3. Spread the mixture on a dehydrator tray lined with a silicone mat to slightly thinner than ⅛ inch. Cut the dough into 1-by-2-inch rectangles.

4. Dehydrate for 12 hours. After about 4 hours of dehydrating, carefully flip the baking mat onto another dehydrator tray and peel the mat from the crackers. Continue dehydrating the crackers until crisp, about 8 hours.

TROUBLESHOOTING: If the bottom of the crackers sticks to the mat when you flip them, dehydrate another 1 to 2 hours before flipping and use an offset metal spatula to ease them off the mat.

PER SERVING (2 CRACKERS) CALORIES: 244; FAT: 21G; CARBS: 7G; SUGAR: 1G; FIBER: 5G; PROTEIN: 1G; SODIUM: 159MG

Coconut Macaroons

YIELD 4 dozen ❈ PREP TIME 15 minutes ❈ DRY TIME 8 to 10 hours

I adore the raw, vegan macaroons sold in the refrigerated section at my local Whole Foods Market, but I do not adore their price tag. So, I decided to make my own. They are fantastic added to lunchboxes or stashed in your office desk drawer in case a snack attack strikes.

4½ cups unsweetened shredded coconut, divided

½ cup maple syrup or agave nectar

1 tablespoon vanilla extract

¼ teaspoon sea salt

1. Preheat the dehydrator to 125°F.

2. Place 3 cups of the coconut in a high-speed blender or food processor. Blend until it begins to form coconut butter, which may take 1 to 2 minutes.

3. Add the maple syrup, vanilla, and sea salt. Blend until smooth.

4. Add the remaining 1½ cups coconut and pulse a few times just until incorporated.

5. Form the mixture into 48 small balls and place them on a dehydrator tray lined with a silicone mat. Flatten with your palm.

6. Dry for 8 to 10 hours, until the macaroons hold together and the exterior is dry to the touch.

INGREDIENT TIP: Use unsweetened shredded coconut in this recipe instead of desiccated coconut. You can usually find it in the health food section or bulk bins of most markets.

PER SERVING (2 MACAROONS) CALORIES: 154; FAT: 12G; CARBS: 9G; SUGAR: 6G; FIBER: 3G; PROTEIN: 2G; SODIUM: 28MG

Oatmeal Raisin Cookies

YIELD 12 to 18 ❋ PREP TIME 10 minutes, plus 30 minutes inactive time
DRY TIME 8 to 12 hours

This recipe starts with a delicious salted date caramel, which acts as a binder and sweetener for the cookies. It is a tasty vegan alternative to eggs and sugar. Feel free to use the caramel in a wide variety of other applications, such as a topping for ice cream or a sweetener for raw vegan desserts.

⅔ cup pitted dates

¼ cup coconut oil, melted

3 tablespoons hot water

2 tablespoons maple syrup
or agave nectar

1 teaspoon vanilla extract or ½ vanilla
bean, split and scraped

¼ teaspoon sea salt

1 cup walnuts

2 cups old-fashioned rolled oats

1 teaspoon ground cinnamon

1½ cups raisins

1. In a large glass measuring cup, combine the dates, coconut oil, hot water, maple syrup, vanilla, and sea salt. Soak the date mixture for about 30 minutes to soften the dates. Purée the date mixture with an immersion blender.

2. Preheat the dehydrator to 135°F.

3. In a food processor or blender, pulse the walnuts a few times until coarsely ground. Add the oats and cinnamon. Pulse a few times more.

4. Pour the date purée into the food processor and blend just until combined. Stir in the raisins.

5. Shape the mixture into 12 to 18 small cookies and put on a dehydrator tray lined with a silicone mat.

6. Dry for 8 to 12 hours, or until the cookies hold together and are dry to the touch but still chewy inside.

INGREDIENT TIP: *For improved digestibility, you can soak the walnuts and oats separately overnight. Rinse and drain thoroughly before adding to the recipe.*

PER SERVING (1 COOKIE) CALORIES: 251; FAT: 12G; CARBS: 35G; SUGAR: 20G; FIBER: 4G; PROTEIN: 5G; SODIUM: 43MG

Salted Chocolate Chip Cookies

YIELD 12 to 18 ❋ PREP TIME 10 minutes, plus 30 minutes inactive time
DRY TIME 8 to 12 hours

Beware—the sea salt in these cookies amps up the flavor of the chocolate and vanilla to create an addictive dessert. Because the recipe is naturally vegan (if you choose vegan chocolate chips), the cookie dough can be eaten raw. But patience pays off and these treats are worth the wait.

⅔ cup pitted dates

¼ cup coconut oil, melted

3 tablespoons hot water

2 tablespoons maple syrup
  or agave nectar

1½ teaspoons vanilla extract or
  1 vanilla bean, split and scraped

½ teaspoon sea salt

3 cups blanched almond flour

1 cup dark chocolate chips

1. In a large measuring cup, combine the dates, coconut oil, hot water, maple syrup, vanilla, and sea salt. Soak the date mixture for about 30 minutes to soften the dates. Purée the date mixture with an immersion blender.

2. Preheat the dehydrator to 135°F.

3. In a food processor or blender, pulse the almond flour a few times until coarsely ground.

4. Pour the date purée into the food processor and blend just until integrated. Stir in the chocolate chips.

5. Shape the mixture into 12 to 18 small cookies and put on a dehydrator tray lined with a silicone mat.

6. Dry for 8 to 12 hours, or until the cookies hold together and are dry to the touch but still chewy inside.

NUTRITIONAL HIGHLIGHT: These cookies are naturally gluten-free, dairy-free, vegan, and Paleo.

PER SERVING (1 COOKIE) CALORIES: 295; FAT: 21G; CARBS: 23G; SUGAR: 14G; FIBER: 4G;
PROTEIN: 7G; SODIUM: 89MG

Pear Crisp

YIELD 4 servings ❖ PREP TIME 10 minutes, plus 4 hours inactive time
DRY TIME 2 hours

I enjoy raw foods most in the summertime when I'm not craving the warmth and comfort that hot foods provide. This pear crisp provides the nostalgic flavors and warmth I adore.

1 cup pecans

6 to 8 pears, unpeeled, cored, and diced

1 vanilla bean, split and scraped

1 tablespoon raw agave nectar

2 teaspoons ground cinnamon, divided

⅛ teaspoon sea salt

½ cup dates

1. In a large jar, combine the pecans with enough water to cover. Place the lid on the jar and soak for at least 4 hours.

2. Preheat the dehydrator to 115°F.

3. In a large bowl, gently toss the pears, vanilla, agave, and 1 teaspoon of the cinnamon to combine. Divide the pears among 4 (6-ounce) ramekins.

4. Thoroughly rinse and drain the pecans. Transfer to a food processor or blender.

5. Add the remaining 1 teaspoon cinnamon, the sea salt, and dates to the food processor. Pulse until mixed but still somewhat chunky. Divide the nut-date mixture among the ramekins to top the pears.

6. Place the ramekins on a dehydrator tray. Dry for 2 hours, until thoroughly warmed.

PREPARATION TIP: This recipe can also be prepared in a single baking dish.

PER SERVING CALORIES: 311; FAT: 6G; CARBS: 70G; SUGAR: 49G; FIBER: 13G; PROTEIN: 3G; SODIUM: 63MG

8

Raw Foods

Juice Pulp Crackers 132

Basic Nut Crackers 133

Raw Flaxseed
Bread 134

Breakfast Crêpes 135

Plantain Cakes with
Raw Sriracha 136

Onion Rings with Raw
Chipotle Aioli 138

Cauliflower Fritters
with Shallots & Balsamic
Syrup 139

Falafel 140

Raw Veggie Pizza 142

Raw Spinach Fettucine
with Tomato Cream
Sauce 144

Fudgy Chocolate-Cherry
Brownies 146

Juice Pulp Crackers

YIELD 1 dozen crackers ❖ PREP TIME 10 minutes ❖ DRY TIME 4 to 6 hours

I love making fresh juices with kale, celery, lime, and apples. It's always such a shame, though, to toss the juice pulp into the compost bin, or, worse, the trash can. These crackers are one of the best uses for juice pulp. Remember to remove inedible skins and seeds from whatever fruit and vegetables you're using before you juice them.

2 cups juice pulp, squeezed
of excess moisture

½ cup ground flaxseed

1 tablespoon extra-virgin olive oil

¼ teaspoon sea salt

1. Preheat the dehydrator to 115°F.

2. In a medium bowl, mix the juice pulp, flaxseed, olive oil, and sea salt with clean hands. Roll out the mixture between a silicone mat and a sheet of parchment paper until it is less than $\frac{1}{8}$ inch thick.

3. With a sharp knife or pizza cutter, cut it into 12 squares.

4. Dry for 4 to 6 hours or until dry and crisp. Store in an airtight container.

PREPARATION TIP: If you do not have a juicer, roughly chop kale, carrots, and celery until you have about 2 cups and put them in a food processor or blender. Pulse until finely chopped. Use your hands or a nut milk bag to squeeze excess moisture from the vegetables before proceeding with the recipe.

INGREDIENT TIP: Use beet juice pulp to make a delicious cracker for goat cheese.

PER SERVING (2 CRACKERS) CALORIES: 104; FAT: 5G; CARBS: 12G; SUGAR: 8G; FIBER: 4G; PROTEIN: 2G; SODIUM: 82MG

Basic Nut Crackers

YIELD 25 (1-inch) crackers ✳ PREP TIME 15 minutes, plus 6 hours inactive time
DRY TIME 8 to 10 hours

This recipe is one of my favorite dehydrated creations. It is vegan and Paleo, making it suitable for all my family and friends. If you have a hankering for a Paleo PB&J, slather one of these crackers with raw almond butter and another with mashed raspberries and prepare to be amazed!

1⅓ cups walnuts

⅓ cup ground flaxseed

2 tablespoons extra-virgin olive oil

1 teaspoon nutritional yeast

½ teaspoon sea salt

½ cup water

¼ cup sunflower seeds

1 tablespoon black sesame seeds

1. Soak the walnuts in enough water to cover for at least 6 hours or overnight. Rinse thoroughly and drain.

2. Preheat the dehydrator to 115°F.

3. In a food processor or blender, blend the soaked nuts, flaxseed, olive oil, nutritional yeast, sea salt, and the water until smooth. In a bowl, combine the mixture with the sunflower seeds and sesame seeds.

4. Spread the mixture about ⅛ inch thick on a dehydrator tray lined with a silicone mat. Cut the dough into 25 (1-inch) squares.

5. Dehydrate for 8 to 10 hours. After about 4 hours of dehydrating, carefully flip the mat onto another dehydrator tray and peel the mat from the crackers. Continue dehydrating for 4 to 6 hours until the crackers are crisp.

TROUBLESHOOTING: If the bottom of the crackers sticks to the mat when you're flipping them, dehydrate for another 1 to 2 hours before flipping and use an offset metal spatula to ease them off the mat.

PER SERVING (2 CRACKERS) CALORIES: 65; FAT: 6G; CARBS: 1G; SUGAR: 0G; FIBER: 1G; PROTEIN: 2G; SODIUM: 40MG

Raw Flaxseed Bread

YIELD 8 slices ❊ PREP TIME 10 minutes ❊ DRY TIME 6 to 8 hours

Whenever I embark on a raw food diet, the most important factor in success is planning ahead. Bread supplies so many elements in the average Western diet—toast for breakfast, sandwiches for lunch, and baguettes with dinner. So, having a supply of this raw vegan bread on hand is important. I know I always have something savory to snack on and that will complement salads and soups.

1 shallot, minced

1 cup ground flaxseed

1 cup water

½ cup almond meal

½ teaspoon sea salt

½ cup roughly chopped shelled pepitas (pumpkin seeds)

¼ cup sesame seeds

¼ cup raisins, finely chopped (optional)

1. Preheat the dehydrator to 115°F.

2. In a large bowl, mix the shallot, flaxseed, water, almond meal, and sea salt until thoroughly combined. Stir in the pepitas, sesame seeds, and raisins (if using).

3. Spread the mixture about $\frac{1}{4}$ inch thick on a dehydrator tray lined with a silicone mat. Cut into 8 pieces.

4. Dehydrate for 3 to 4 hours until no longer sticky. Flip the mat onto a separate dehydrator tray. Remove the mat and dehydrate for another 3 to 4 hours, or until soft and spongy.

NUTRITIONAL HIGHLIGHT: Raw foods are naturally gluten-free and Paleo. Even if you don't follow a raw diet, this bread is great to have on hand for other dietary needs.

PER SERVING (1 SLICE) CALORIES: 153; FAT: 11G; CARBS: 7G; SUGAR: 0G; FIBER: 5G; PROTEIN: 6G; SODIUM: 123MG

Breakfast Crêpes

YIELD 6 to 8 crêpes ❖ PREP TIME 10 minutes ❖ DRY TIME 6 to 8 hours

Although it took some courage, breaking into my first young coconut was such a revelation. The meat is soft and sweet and fresh coconut water is exquisite! It is full of electrolytes, vitamins, and minerals, and knocks the socks off canned varieties. Serve these crêpes with raw macadamia nut cheese (see Tip) and fresh berries.

2 young coconuts, meat only

2 tablespoons agave nectar
   or maple syrup

1 vanilla bean, split and scraped

Pinch of sea salt

1. Preheat the dehydrator to 115°F.

2. In a blender, purée the coconut meat, agave nectar, tiny vanilla seeds, and sea salt until smooth.

3. Pour ¼-cup portions of batter on the dehydrator trays lined with silicone mats. Smooth the batter into circles.

4. Dry for 6 to 8 hours, or until the crêpes are completely set and peel easily from the mat.

COOKING TIP: To make macadamia nut cheese, soak the nuts in water for at least 4 hours. Rinse and drain. Purée in a blender with fresh lemon juice, a pinch of sea salt, and sweeten with agave nectar. Add water, as needed, to blend.

PER SERVING (2 CRÊPES) CALORIES: 107; FAT: 3G; CARBS: 19G; SUGAR: 12G; FIBER: 0G; PROTEIN: 1G; SODIUM: 66MG

Plantain Cakes with Raw Sriracha

YIELD 6 to 8 cakes ✣ PREP TIME 10 minutes, plus 10 minutes inactive time
DRY TIME 6 to 7 hours

I first tried the Puerto Rican dish mofongo at a sunny restaurant in Venice, California, after a day of surfing. Since then, I just can't get enough of the flavor combination, especially the way it was prepared with shaved fennel. Here's my raw, vegan take on the dish. It makes a delicious breakfast or nice appetizer.

FOR THE SAUCE

4 garlic cloves

1 tablespoon cayenne pepper

¼ teaspoon sea salt

¼ cup raw agave nectar

2 tablespoons apple cider vinegar

FOR THE PLANTAIN CAKES

2 ripe yellow plantains, peeled and cut into chunks

2 garlic cloves, divided

2 tablespoons coconut oil, melted

¼ teaspoon sea salt

½ cup warm water

2 tablespoons ground flaxseed

½ cup very thinly sliced fennel bulb

½ cup roughly chopped fresh cilantro

To make the sauce

1. Use a Microplane grater to grate the garlic, or mince it finely, and put in a small bowl.

2. Whisk in the cayenne pepper, sea salt, agave nectar, and vinegar. Set aside.

To make the plantain cakes

3. Preheat the dehydrator to 115°F.

4. In a blender, pulse the plantains, garlic cloves, coconut oil, and sea salt until thoroughly combined, adding some of the warm water as needed to keep things moving. Add the flaxseed and fennel and mix until combined. Allow the mixture to rest for 10 minutes.

5. Scoop the plantain batter into 6 to 8 small cakes and put onto a dehydrator tray lined with a silicone mat.

6. Dry for 4 hours. Flip the cakes and dry for another 2 to 3 hours, or until warm and dry to the touch.

7. To serve, place a few plantain cakes on a serving dish and drizzle with the sauce, or put the sauce in a small shallow bowl for dipping.

8. Sprinkle with fresh cilantro.

PREPARATION TIP: If you want to use some of your own dried chiles in this recipe, dried chiles de árbol make a great substitution for the cayenne pepper, but they should be ground.

PER SERVING (1 CAKE) CALORIES: 145; FAT: 6G; CARBS: 25G; SUGAR: 12G; FIBER: 3G; PROTEIN: 2G; SODIUM: 164MG

Onion Rings
with Raw Chipotle Aioli

YIELD 48 rings ✳ PREP TIME 10 minutes, plus 1 hour inactive time
DRY TIME 10 to 12 hours

Traditional deep-fried onion rings are really not a vegetable. (Admit it.) These raw onion rings, however, are crunchy, flavorful, and addicting, especially when dipped in the chipotle aioli.

FOR THE ONION RINGS

1½ cups ground flaxseed

½ teaspoon ground cumin

½ teaspoon ground coriander

½ teaspoon sea salt

¼ cup extra-virgin olive oil

2 yellow onions, cut in ¼-inch rings, separated

FOR THE CHIPOTLE AIOLI

1 cup macadamia nuts

½ cup water, plus more for soaking

1 tablespoon freshly squeezed lemon juice

1 garlic clove, minced

1 teaspoon ground chipotle

To make the onion rings

1. Preheat the dehydrator to 115°F.

2. In a small bowl, stir together the flaxseed, cumin, coriander, and sea salt.

3. Put the olive oil in another small bowl. Dip the onion rings in the olive oil and then dredge in the flaxseed mixture.

4. Put the onion rings on the dehydrator trays. Dry for 10 to 12 hours, or until soft and crispy.

To make the chipotle aioli

1. At least 1 hour before the onions are dry, put the macadamia nuts in a large jar and cover with fresh water. Soak for at least 1 hour. Rinse and drain.

2. In a blender, blend the macadamia nuts, ½ cup water, lemon juice, garlic, and chipotle until smooth. Pour the aoli in a small serving bowl.

INGREDIENT TIP: If you cannot find ground chipotle, use smoked paprika or another ground chile pepper.

PER SERVING (6 RINGS) CALORIES: 298; FAT: 26G; CARBS: 11G; SUGAR: 8G; FIBER: 2G; PROTEIN: 6G; SODIUM: 126MG

Cauliflower Fritters with Shallots & Balsamic Syrup

YIELD 12 fritters ✳ PREP TIME 10 minutes ✳ DRY TIME 6 to 8 hours

These fritters offer the perfect balance of salty, sour, and sweet. They make a perfect raw dinner with a simple salad.

1 (2-pound) cauliflower

½ cup ground flaxseed

¼ cup minced fresh parsley,
  plus more for serving

2 garlic cloves, minced

Zest of 1 lemon

½ teaspoon sea salt

4 shallots, cut into thin rings

¼ cup raw agave nectar

¼ cup balsamic vinegar

1. Preheat the dehydrator to 115°F.

2. Shred the cauliflower in a food processor fitted with a grater attachment or finely chop the cauliflower with a knife. Transfer to a large bowl.

3. Add the flaxseed, parsley, garlic, lemon zest, and sea salt. Form the mixture into 12 small cakes and place them on a dehydrator tray.

4. Dry for 6 to 8 hours, until warmed and set.

5. To make the shallot balsamic syrup, place the shallots in a small bowl.

6. In another small bowl, whisk the agave nectar and balsamic vinegar. Pour 2 tablespoons of this syrup over the shallots and toss gently to combine. During the last 2 hours of drying, spread the shallots on a dehydrator tray lined with a silicone mat and dry with the cauliflower.

7. To serve, carefully place the cauliflower fritters onto individual serving plates, top with the shallots, drizzle with the remaining balsamic syrup, and sprinkle with fresh parsley.

PER SERVING (1 FRITTER) CALORIES: 55; FAT: 2G; CARBS: 9G; SUGAR: 6G; FIBER: 2G; PROTEIN: 2G; SODIUM: 87MG

Falafel

YIELD 12 ❈ PREP TIME 15 minutes ❈ DRY TIME 2 hours

I love the bright flavor of the vegetables in this Middle Eastern dish. This version is far healthier than traditional fried falafel balls made with chickpeas. It is especially good served with a drizzle of tahini and a salad of grape tomatoes, parsley, and shallots.

1 cup vegetable juice pulp, from juiced kale, carrots, and celery

½ cup ground pistachios or walnuts

½ red onion, minced

¼ cup minced fresh parsley

¼ cup minced fresh cilantro

2 tablespoons ground flaxseed

2 tablespoons sesame seeds

1 garlic clove, minced

1 teaspoon ground cumin

1 teaspoon ground coriander

½ teaspoon sea salt

1. Preheat the dehydrator to 115°F.

2. In a food processor or blender, combine the vegetable juice pulp, pistachios, red onion, parsley, cilantro, flaxseed, sesame seeds, garlic, cumin, coriander, and sea salt. Pulse until fully mixed but not uniform in texture.

3. Shape the mixture into 12 (1-inch) balls and place them on the dehydrator trays.

4. Dry for 2 hours, or until warm and dry.

PER SERVING CALORIES: 55; FAT: 42G; CARBS: 3G; SUGAR: 1G; FIBER: 1G; PROTEIN: 2G; SODIUM: 87MG

Raw Veggie Pizza

YIELD 2 servings ✤ PREP TIME 20 minutes, plus 30 minutes inactive time
DRY TIME 7 to 9

Pizza is the holy grail of raw food. I've found that keeping it simple is the best solution for recreating the classic pie. Fresh herbs, ripe tomatoes, and a few simple toppings do the trick. Garnish with nut "Parmesan" (see Cooking Tip for a recipe) to finish.

FOR THE CRUST

1 recipe Raw Flaxseed Bread (page 134) batter, prepared *without pepitas* and *raisins*

FOR THE PIZZA TOPPINGS

1 small zucchini, cut into thin rounds

1 cup sliced mushrooms

½ red onion, very thinly sliced

½ cup fresh basil, cut into chiffonade

Nut "Parmesan" cheese (see Tip; optional)

FOR THE SAUCE

2 cups roughly chopped fresh tomatoes

2 tablespoons extra-virgin olive oil

1 pitted date, soaked in warm water for 10 minutes

1 garlic clove, minced

1 tablespoon minced onion

1 teaspoon dried oregano (see Herbs: Perennial, page 87)

1 teaspoon red wine vinegar

Sea salt

Freshly ground black pepper

To make the crust

1. Preheat the dehydrator to 115°F.

2. Pour the Raw Flaxseed Bread batter on a dehydrator tray lined with a silicone mat. Spread it into a circle, about ½ to ¼ inch thick, to form a crust. Do not slice it. Dehydrate for 3 to 4 hours until no longer sticky. Carefully flip the crust onto a separate dehydrator tray and dehydrate for 2 to 3 hours more, or until soft and spongy.

To make the sauce

1. About 30 minutes before flipping the crust, make the sauce. In a blender, purée the tomatoes, olive oil, date (discard the soaking liquid), garlic, onion, oregano, and vinegar until smooth. Season with sea salt and pepper. Transfer the tomato mixture to a nut milk bag or a fine-mesh sieve lined with cheesecloth. Let drain for 30 minutes to remove any excess liquid.

2. When you flip the crust for its second drying time, spread the sauce on a dehydrator tray lined with a silicone mat. Put it in the dehydrator with the crust and dry for 2 to 3 hours until thickened and warm. The sauce and the crust will be done at the same time.

To finish the pizza

1. Scrape the sauce off the silicone mat, and spread it over the crust. Top with zucchini, mushrooms, onion, and basil.

2. Dry for 2 hours more, or until all ingredients are warmed.

3. Sprinkle with nut "Parmesan" cheese (if using).

COOKING TIP: Create a simple nut "Parmesan" cheese to top this pizza. In a food processor or blender, combine 1 cup macadamia nuts with $\frac{1}{4}$ cup nutritional yeast, 1 teaspoon sea salt, and 1 teaspoon garlic powder. Blend until the mixture resembles coarse sand. Sprinkle over the finished pizza. Refrigerate leftovers in a covered container.

PER SERVING CALORIES: 741; FAT: 53G; CARBS: 44G; SUGAR: 12G; FIBER: 25G; PROTEIN: 23G; SODIUM: 509MG

Raw Spinach Fettucine with Tomato Cream Sauce

YIELD 2 servings ❖ PREP TIME 15 minutes, plus 1 hour inactive time
DRY TIME 3 to 4 hours

Raw vegan recipes often call for spiralized vegetable noodles, usually zucchini. The veggie noodles are simple and tasty, but sometimes I prefer a texture more akin to pasta. This pasta dough fills the bill and the tomato cream sauce is absolutely delectable.

FOR THE FETTUCINE

2 cups young coconut meat

1 cup loosely packed fresh baby spinach

¼ cup ground flaxseed

1 garlic clove

¼ teaspoon sea salt

FOR THE SAUCE

1 cup macadamia nuts

½ cup dried Tomatoes (page 98)

½ cup warm water, plus more as needed

2 tablespoons extra-virgin olive oil

1 garlic clove

1 teaspoon nutritional yeast

¼ teaspoon sea salt

Pinch of red pepper flakes

FOR ASSEMBLING THE DISH

1 tablespoon minced fresh basil, for garnishing

Nut "Parmesan" cheese (see Cooking Tip, page 143) for garnish (optional)

To make the fettucine

1. Preheat the dehydrator to 115°F.

2. In a blender, purée the coconut, spinach, flaxseed, garlic, and sea salt until smooth.

3. Spread the coconut mixture about ⅛ inch thick on a dehydrator tray lined with a silicone mat.

4. Dry for 2 to 3 hours. Flip the "pasta sheet" over. With a pizza cutter or a sharp knife, cut the pasta sheet into long, thin strips about ¼ inch wide. Dry for 1 hour more, or until warm, soft, and chewy.

To make the sauce

1. While the crust is drying, in a small bowl, soak the macadamia nuts in water for at least 1 hour.

2. In another small bowl, soak the tomatoes in ½ cup warm water for at least 1 hour.

3. Drain and rinse the macadamia nuts. Transfer them to a blender. Add the tomatoes and their soaking liquid, the olive oil, garlic, nutritional yeast, sea salt, and red pepper flakes. Purée until smooth, adding more warm water as needed to produce a creamy texture.

4. Just before serving, purée the sauce on high for about 1 minute, which will warm it gently.

To assemble the dish

Divide the noodles between 2 serving dishes. Top with the tomato sauce. Garnish with a pinch of fresh basil and sprinkle with nut "Parmesan" (if using).

PER SERVING CALORIES: 792; FAT: 72G; CARBS: 34G; SUGAR: 14G; FIBER: 12G; PROTEIN: 12G; SODIUM: 792MG

Fudgy Chocolate-Cherry Brownies

YIELD 8 brownies ❋ PREP TIME 10 minutes, plus 6 hours inactive time
DRY TIME 8 to 12 hours

If you love traditional brownies but not traditional preparations, get ready to be amazed. These ooey, gooey little morsels of chocolaty goodness take the cake. (Sorry, couldn't resist.) And—bonus—they're actually good for you! They are adapted from the book Living Raw Food *by Sarma Melngailis.*

1 cup walnuts

¾ cup maple syrup

½ cup water

1 teaspoon vanilla extract

1½ cups blanched almond flour

1 cup good-quality cocoa powder

¼ teaspoon sea salt

1 cup dried Cherries (page 51; optional)

1. Soak the walnuts in enough water to cover for at least 6 hours or overnight. Rinse and drain thoroughly.

2. Preheat the dehydrator to 125°F.

3. In a blender, purée the soaked walnuts, maple syrup, water, and vanilla until very smooth.

4. Add the almond flour, cocoa powder, and sea salt. Blend, scraping down the sides of the bowl to mix everything thoroughly. Fold in the cherries (if using).

5. Spread the mixture about 1 inch thick on a dehydrator tray lined with a silicone mat.

6. Dry for 8 to 12 hours, or until the brownies are dry to the touch and easy to lift from the mat with a metal spatula.

COOKING TIP: To make these brownies raw, reduce the dehydrator temperature to 120°F, and use almond meal (instead of flour), raw cocoa powder, raw agave nectar instead of maple syrup, and 1 vanilla bean, split and scraped.

PER SERVING (1 BROWNIE) CALORIES: 325; FAT: 21G; CARBS: 32G; SUGAR: 18G; FIBER: 7G;
PROTEIN: 10G; SODIUM: 72MG

PART FOUR

RECIPES *with* DEHYDRATED INGREDIENTS

CHAPTER NINE
Breakfast

CHAPTER TEN
Soups

CHAPTER ELEVEN
Vegetarian & Vegan Entrées

CHAPTER TWELVE
Meat & Poultry Entrées

CHAPTER THIRTEEN
Desserts

Breakfast

Power Greens
Smoothie 152

Berry Blast
Smoothie 153

Tropical Breeze
Smoothie 154

Vegan Blueberry-Apple
Muffins 155

Pumpkin Bread 156

Zucchini Bread 157

Morning Glory
Muffins 158

Berry-Almond
Granola 159

Grain-Free Fruit &
Nut Granola 160

Salted Chocolate
Cranberry Bars 162

Vanilla-Peach Slow
Cooker Oatmeal 163

Fruity Quinoa Pilaf 164

Veggie Breakfast
Casserole 165

Power Greens Smoothie

YIELD 2 servings ❋ PREP TIME 5 minutes

This smoothie recipe is great for those days when you don't have the time to rinse and chop fresh vegetables but still want the vitamins and minerals of dark leafy greens. I like the flavor of kale in my smoothies, but you can also use dried spinach, Swiss chard, or whichever green you prefer.

1 cup almond milk

1 ripe mango, peeled, pitted, and diced

¼ cup dried Kale (page 89), ground into a fine powder

2 peeled, frozen ripe bananas, cut into chunks

In a blender, in this order, layer the almond milk, mango, kale powder, and bananas. Pulse a few times to get things moving, then purée until smooth.

PER SERVING CALORIES: 197; FAT: 2G; CARBS: 46G; SUGAR: 30G; FIBER: 6G; PROTEIN: 3G; SODIUM: 82MG

Berry Blast Smoothie

YIELD 2 servings ❋ PREP TIME 5 minutes, plus 30 minutes inactive time

Enjoy the flavors of fresh berries, whatever the season, in this sweet and fruity smoothie. If you prefer a nondairy beverage, use nondairy milk and yogurt, such as almond- or coconut-based products.

¼ cup dried Blueberries (page 50)

¼ cup dried Cherries (page 51)

1 cup plain yogurt

1 tablespoon dried Raspberries
 (page 67), ground into a fine powder

¼ teaspoon vanilla extract

1 cup crushed ice

½ cup milk

1. In a jar, combine the blueberries and cherries with enough water to cover. Let sit to rehydrate for at least 30 minutes.

2. Pour the blueberries and cherries and their soaking water into a blender.

3. Add the yogurt, raspberry powder, and vanilla. Pulse a few times and then add the crushed ice. Purée until smooth, adding the milk as needed to thin out the smoothie.

TROUBLESHOOTING: Measure the raspberries after they have been ground and sifted. For a smoother texture, sift the ground raspberries to remove the seeds before you add the powder to the smoothie.

PER SERVING CALORIES: 150; FAT: 3G; CARBS: 20G; SUGAR: 17G; FIBER: 1G; PROTEIN: 10G; SODIUM: 115MG

Tropical Breeze Smoothie

YIELD 2 servings ❈ PREP TIME 5 minutes, plus 1 hour inactive time

I love mango and pineapple in my smoothies, but cutting and peeling them fresh is time-consuming on busy mornings. With a little planning, I can rehydrate my dried supply in the refrigerator overnight and breakfast comes together quickly! The coconut milk offers a hint of the tropics and is naturally vegan, but, if you prefer, you can use plain Greek yogurt.

1 cup dried Mango (page 59)

½ cup dried Pineapple (page 65)

1 cup water

1 tablespoon freshly squeezed lime juice

½ cup coconut milk or plain Greek yogurt

1 peeled and frozen banana,
   cut into chunks

½ cup crushed ice

1. In a jar, combine the mango, pineapple, and water. Place the lid on the jar and refrigerate for at least 1 hour or overnight to rehydrate.

2. In a blender, put the rehydrated mango, pineapple, and any remaining soaking liquid, and add the lime juice, coconut milk, banana, and crushed ice and purée until smooth.

PREPARATION TIP: *At the beginning of the week, fill several small mason jars with dried fruit to make this smoothie come together even more quickly. Simply add water before you go to bed and blend in the morning.*

PER SERVING CALORIES: 134; FAT: 4G; CARBS: 25G; SUGAR: 15G; FIBER: 2G; PROTEIN: 3G; SODIUM: 39MG

Vegan Blueberry-Apple Muffins

YIELD 12 muffins ❋ PREP TIME 10 minutes ❋ COOK TIME 20 to 25 minutes

Dried blueberries can be used in virtually any blueberry muffin or pancake recipe. I'm partial to this one because it is vegan and can be easily converted to gluten-free. The applesauce and dried apples increase the sweetness while keeping the added sugar to a minimum.

1½ cups whole-wheat pastry flour

2 teaspoons baking powder

½ teaspoon baking soda

½ teaspoon sea salt

⅓ cup evaporated cane juice

½ cup applesauce

½ cup almond milk

½ cup melted coconut oil or canola oil

1 whisked "flax egg" (see Tip)

1 cup dried Blueberries (page 50)

1 cup dried Apples (page 46), diced

1. Preheat the oven to 325°F.

2. Line a standard 12-cup muffin tin with paper liners.

3. In a large bowl, sift the flour, baking powder, baking soda, sea salt, and evaporated cane juice. Make a well in the center of the flour mixture. Add the applesauce, almond milk, coconut oil, and "flax egg." Stir just until mixed.

4. Fold in the dried blueberries and apples.

5. Divide the batter among the muffin cups. Bake for 20 to 25 minutes, or until the tops are golden brown and a toothpick inserted in the center comes out clean.

PREPARATION TIP: To make the "flax egg," whisk 1 tablespoon ground flaxseed with 1 tablespoon water. Let rest for 5 minutes before using.

SUBSTITUTION TIP: To make this recipe gluten-free, swap the whole-wheat pastry flour for 1 cup of brown rice flour, ¼ cup tapioca starch, and ¼ cup potato starch or another gluten-free flour blend.

PER SERVING (1 MUFFIN) CALORIES: 181; FAT: 12G; CARBS: 19G; SUGAR: 5G; FIBER: 1G; PROTEIN: 2G; SODIUM: 136 MG

Pumpkin Bread

YIELD 1 loaf (12 slices) ❋ PREP TIME 10 minutes, plus 2 hours inactive time
COOK TIME 1 hour

This recipe is a lightened-up version of my mother-in-law Debbie's pumpkin bread recipe. She says there is no such thing as too much ground cinnamon, and I tend to agree. The flavor of the olive oil complements the pumpkin with just a hint of flavor in the finished bread. Instead of pumpkin, you can use acorn squash, butternut squash, or kabocha squash if you want.

1 cup dried pumpkin
  (Squash, page 97)

1 cup unsweetened apple juice

½ cup packed brown sugar

2 large eggs, whisked

½ cup extra-virgin olive oil

2 cups whole-wheat pastry flour

1 tablespoon ground cinnamon

1 teaspoon ground dried Ginger
  (page 83)

1 teaspoon baking soda

½ teaspoon sea salt

1 cup dried Grapes (page 57),
  or commercial raisins

1 cup roughly chopped dried walnuts
  (Nuts & Seeds, page 62)

1. In a large jar, stir together the pumpkin and apple juice. Refrigerate to rehydrate for at least 2 hours or up to overnight. When the pumpkin is soft to the touch, purée it in a blender or food processor.

2. Preheat the oven to 350°F.

3. Line a 9-by-5-inch loaf pan with parchment paper.

4. In a large bowl, whisk the pumpkin purée, brown sugar, eggs, and olive oil.

5. In a separate bowl, sift the flour, cinnamon, ginger, baking soda, and sea salt. Add the flour mixture to the pumpkin mixture and stir just until combined.

6. Fold in the raisins and walnuts.

7. Pour the batter into the prepared loaf pan. Bake for 1 hour, or until a toothpick inserted in the center comes out clean.

SUBSTITUTION TIP: For a special treat, swap the raisins and walnuts for 1½ cups roughly chopped bittersweet chocolate.

PER SERVING (1 SLICE) CALORIES: 301; FAT: 16G; CARBS: 37G; SUGAR: 16G; FIBER: 3G; PROTEIN: 6G; SODIUM: 199MG

Zucchini Bread

YIELD 1 loaf (12 slices) ❋ PREP TIME 10 minutes ❋ COOK TIME 45 to 55 minutes

Most zucchini bread recipes ask you to squeeze all the excess moisture out of the zucchini before folding it into the batter. With dried zucchini, this step is already done. You can also use dried lemon zest instead of fresh if you have some on hand.

1½ cups whole-wheat pastry flour

½ cup packed brown sugar

1 teaspoon ground cinnamon

1 teaspoon baking soda

½ teaspoon sea salt

¼ teaspoon freshly ground nutmeg

2 large eggs, whisked

½ cup melted coconut oil or canola oil

Zest of 1 lemon

Juice of 1 lemon

1 cup dried shredded Zucchini (page 99)

½ cup roughly chopped dried pecans (see Nuts & Seeds, page 62)

1. Preheat the oven to 350°F.

2. Line a 9-by-5-inch loaf pan with parchment paper.

3. In a large bowl, sift the flour, brown sugar, cinnamon, baking soda, sea salt, and nutmeg.

4. Make a well in the center of the flour mixture. Stir in the eggs, coconut oil, lemon zest, and lemon juice just until mixed. Fold in the dried zucchini and pecans.

5. Pour the batter into the prepared pan. Bake for 45 to 55 minutes, or until the top is golden brown and a toothpick inserted in the center comes out clean.

PER SERVING (1 SLICE) CALORIES: 180; FAT: 11G; CARBS: 19G; SUGAR: 6G; FIBER: 1G; PROTEIN: 3G; SODIUM: 197MG

Morning Glory Muffins

YIELD 12 muffins ❖ PREP TIME 10 minutes ❖ COOK TIME 20 to 25 minutes

I grew up enjoying morning glory muffins. They are delicious made with fresh or dehydrated ingredients. Feel free to substitute other dried fruits and vegetables, letting your imagination and your pantry guide your choices.

1⅓ cups whole-wheat pastry flour

⅓ cup packed brown sugar

1½ teaspoons baking soda

1 teaspoon ground cinnamon

½ teaspoon sea salt

2 large eggs, whisked

½ cup melted coconut oil or canola oil

½ cup warm water

1 teaspoon vanilla extract

½ cup dried diced Apples (page 46)

½ cup shredded dried Carrots (page 76)

½ cup dried Grapes (page 57)

½ cup dried walnuts (see Nuts & Seeds, page 62)

1. Preheat the oven to 325°F.

2. Line a standard 12-cup muffin tin with paper liners.

3. In a large bowl, sift the flour, brown sugar, baking soda, cinnamon, and sea salt. Make a well in the center of the ingredients.

4. Add the eggs, coconut oil, water, and vanilla. Stir just until mixed.

5. Fold in the dried apples, carrots, grapes, and walnuts.

6. Divide the batter among the 12 muffin cups. Bake for 20 to 25 minutes, or until the tops are gently browned and a toothpick inserted in the center comes out clean.

PER SERVING (1 MUFFIN) CALORIES: 220; FAT: 13 G; CARBS: 23G; SUGAR: 8G; FIBER: 1G; PROTEIN: 4G; SODIUM: 254MG

Berry-Almond Granola

YIELD 7 cups ❖ PREP TIME 10 minutes
COOK TIME 20 minutes, plus 10 minutes resting time

The sweetness of the dried cherries and blueberries makes this healthy breakfast recipe almost like a dessert. I like to serve it with fresh or frozen berries over plain yogurt. It's also good as a topping for ice cream.

2 cups old-fashioned rolled oats

1 cup roughly chopped dried almonds
(see Nuts & Seeds, page 62)

1 cup shredded, unsweetened dried
Coconut (page 53)

½ cup honey or maple syrup

¼ cup melted coconut oil or canola oil

1 teaspoon vanilla extract

¼ teaspoon sea salt

1 cup dried Cherries (page 51)

1 cup dried Blueberries (page 50)

1. Preheat the oven to 325°F.

2. In a large bowl, mix the oats, almonds, and coconut.

3. In a small bowl, whisk the honey, coconut oil, vanilla, and sea salt. Pour over the oat mixture and stir until thoroughly combined.

4. Spread the mixture into a rimmed baking sheet. Bake for 10 minutes. Stir and bake for 10 minutes more. Stir again. Turn off the oven. Leave the pan in the oven for 10 minutes.

5. Stir in the cherries and blueberries. Store in an airtight container.

PER SERVING (½ CUP) CALORIES: 212; FAT: 13G; CARBS: 23G; SUGAR: 12G; FIBER: 3G; PROTEIN: 4G; SODIUM: 39MG

Grain-Free Fruit & Nut Granola

YIELD 5 cups ✻ PREP TIME 10 minutes
COOK TIME 20 minutes, plus 20 to 30 minutes resting time

A grain-free diet provides many people, myself included, relief from allergies, more energy, better sleep, and improved digestion. These benefits notwithstanding, the hankering for cold breakfast cereal remains. This simple fruit and nut granola satisfies every time and keeps me full until lunchtime.

2 cups dried Nuts and Seeds (page 62)

1 cup shredded, unsweetened dried Coconut (page 53)

¼ cup honey or maple syrup

¼ cup coconut oil, melted

1 teaspoon ground cinnamon

Pinch of sea salt

1 cup dried Grapes (page 57)

1 cup roughly chopped dried Apples (page 46)

1. Preheat the oven to 325°F.

2. In a food processor or blender, pulse the nuts and seeds until coarsely ground. Transfer to a large bowl and stir in the coconut.

3. In a small bowl, whisk the honey, coconut oil, cinnamon, and sea salt. Pour over the nuts and coconut and stir until thoroughly combined.

4. Spread the mixture into a rimmed baking sheet. Bake for 10 minutes. Stir and bake for 10 minutes more. Stir again. Turn off the oven. Leave the baking sheet in the oven for 20 to 30 minutes until the mixture is crisp and dry.

5. Stir in the dried grapes and apples. Store in an airtight container.

PER SERVING (½ CUP) CALORIES: 349; FAT: 27G; CARBS: 25G; SUGAR: 18G; FIBER: 4G; PROTEIN: 7G; SODIUM: 30MG

Salted Chocolate Cranberry Bars

YIELD 16 (4-inch) bars ❖ PREP TIME 5 minutes ❖ COOK TIME 2 minutes

Sea salt and dark chocolate are my undoing. I especially love them in these simple, vegan refrigerator energy bars. The tartness of dried cranberries provides yet another layer of delicious.

1 cup dried almonds (see Nuts & Seeds, page 62)

1 cup shredded, unsweetened, dried Coconut (page 53)

1 cup dried Cranberries (page 54)

1 cup roughly chopped bittersweet chocolate

½ cup almond butter

¼ cup maple syrup

½ teaspoon sea salt

1. Line an 8-by-8-inch baking pan with parchment paper.

2. In a food processor or blender, pulse the almonds, coconut, and cranberries until coarsely ground. Transfer to a large bowl and stir in the chocolate.

3. In a small skillet over medium-low heat, whisk the almond butter and maple syrup. Bring almost to a simmer and then remove from the heat.

4. Pour the almond butter mixture over the nut and fruit mixture. It will partially melt the chocolate, but some pieces will remain intact. Stir gently to mix.

5. Pour the batter into the prepared pan, pressing it down with the back of a fork. Sprinkle the top with the sea salt.

6. Refrigerate until set, about 3 hours. Slice into 16 bars.

PER SERVING (1 BAR) CALORIES: 202; FAT: 15G; CARBS: 14G; SUGAR: 9G; FIBER: 3G; PROTEIN: 4G; SODIUM: 70MG

Vanilla-Peach
Slow Cooker Oatmeal

YIELD 2 to 4 servings ❋ PREP TIME 5 minutes ❋ COOK TIME 8 hours

When left to rehydrate overnight, the sweet flavors of dried peaches and dates permeate this oatmeal. You can also prepare this on the stovetop in just a few minutes. Simply use old-fashioned rolled oats instead of steel cut oats and bring to a simmer over medium-low heat. Cover and cook on low for 5 minutes.

1 teaspoon melted butter or melted
   coconut oil

1 cup steel cut oats

1 cup roughly chopped dried Peaches
   (see Nectarines & Peaches, page 61)

¼ cup finely dried diced Dates (page 55)

1 teaspoon vanilla extract

¼ teaspoon ground nutmeg

Pinch of sea salt

4 cups water

1. Coat the interior of the slow cooker crock with butter. Add the oats, peaches, dates, vanilla, nutmeg, and sea salt. Pour in the water, stirring gently to mix.

2. Cover and cook for 8 hours on low.

SUBSTITUTION TIP: Swap the peaches for any of the delicious dried fruits in chapter 4 (page 45). Some of my favorites for this use are apples, bananas, apricots, pears, and cherries.

PER SERVING CALORIES: 275; FAT: 5G; CARBS: 53G; SUGAR: 22G; FIBER: 7G; PROTEIN: 7G; SODIUM: 134MG

Fruity Quinoa Pilaf

YIELD 4 servings ❋ PREP TIME 15 minutes ❋ COOK TIME 20 minutes

Quinoa might seem like a strange food for breakfast, but it has such a neutral flavor, it easily transforms into a warm and filling porridge or a yummy fruit salad. This recipe leans more toward a fruit salad. It also makes a fantastic vegan lunch served over a bed of arugula.

2 cups apple juice or water

1 cup quinoa, rinsed and drained

¼ cup dried diced Pineapple (page 65)

2 tablespoons coconut oil, melted

1 tablespoon freshly squeezed lime juice

1 tablespoon agave nectar

1 cup fresh blueberries

1 cup fresh grapes, halved

¼ cup slivered dried Kiwi (page 58)

¼ cup shredded dried Coconut (page 53)

½ cup chopped dried pecans (see Nuts & Seeds, page 62)

1. In a medium saucepan over medium heat, bring the apple juice, quinoa, and pineapple to a simmer. Cover, reduce the heat to low, and cook for about 20 minutes until tender. Fluff with a fork and transfer to a serving bowl to cool.

2. In a small bowl, whisk the coconut oil, lime juice, and agave nectar. Drizzle over the quinoa.

3. Add the blueberries, grapes, and dried kiwi to the quinoa. Toss gently to mix.

4. Divide the quinoa among 4 serving plates. Sprinkle with the coconut and pecans.

PREPARATION TIP: For even more flavor and a nice crunchy texture, toast the coconut in a dry skillet over medium heat for 3 to 4 minutes, until gently browned and fragrant.

PER SERVING CALORIES: 402; FAT: 16G; CARBS: 59G; SUGAR: 26G; FIBER: 6G; PROTEIN: 8G; SODIUM: 10MG

Veggie Breakfast Casserole

YIELD 4 servings ❖ PREP TIME 5 minutes, plus 8 hours inactive time
COOK TIME 30 minutes, plus 10 minutes resting time

I love the idea of breakfast casseroles. Typically when I wake up, though, I'm not very interested in preparing a full meal. My simple solution to this dilemma is to make the casserole the night before. This works especially well with dehydrated ingredients because they can rehydrate overnight.

1 teaspoon extra-virgin olive oil
   or butter

½ cup dried sliced Zucchini (page 99)

½ cup dried sliced Tomatoes (page 98)

½ cup dried sliced Mushrooms
   (page 91)

¼ cup dried diced Onions (page 92)

8 large eggs

1 cup milk

½ cup shredded Parmesan cheese

1 teaspoon dried thyme
   (see Herbs: Perennial, page 87)

¼ teaspoon sea salt

⅛ teaspoon freshly ground
   black pepper

1. Coat the interior of an 8-by-8-inch baking dish with olive oil.

2. Layer the zucchini, tomatoes, mushrooms, and onions in the dish.

3. In a large bowl, whisk the eggs. Add the milk, Parmesan cheese, thyme, sea salt, and pepper. Whisk again to mix. Pour the egg mixture over the vegetables. Cover the baking dish tightly with aluminum foil and refrigerate at least 8 hours.

4. Preheat the oven to 350°F.

5. Bake the casserole for 20 minutes. Remove the foil and continue baking until lightly browned and set, about 10 minutes more. Allow to rest for 10 minutes before cutting and serving.

SUBSTITUTION TIP: If you prefer a nondairy casserole, use coconut milk or unsweetened almond milk and omit the cheese.

PER SERVING CALORIES: 254; FAT: 16G; CARBS: 10G; SUGAR: 7G; FIBER: 1G; PROTEIN: 21G; SODIUM: 561MG

Soups

Vegetable Broth Mix 168

Cream of Tomato Soup 169

Mint & Pea Soup 170

Corn Chowder 171

French Onion Soup 172

Cream of Mushroom Soup 174

Cream of Celery Soup 175

Minestrone Soup 176

Broccoli-Cheddar Bisque 177

Borscht 178

Creamy Cauliflower Soup 179

Kale & White Bean Soup 180

Carrot-Ginger-Orange Soup 182

Leek & Potato Soup 183

Vegetable Broth Mix

YIELD 4 cups ✱ PREP TIME 10 minutes

I haven't bought commercially prepared broth or stock in several years since I learned to make it myself. Typically, I save vegetable scraps for a few weeks in the freezer until I have enough to make broth and I need it for a recipe. Dehydrating it is even better because the powder is ready instantly and can be stored in the cupboard, not the freezer. It also lets you control the amount of liquid, if you use this powder stirred into other sauces.

1 cup shredded dried Carrots (page 76)

1 cup dried diced Celery (page 78)

1 cup dried diced Onions (page 92)

½ cup dried diced bell Peppers (page 94)

½ cup dried sliced Mushrooms (page 91)

¼ cup dried Tomatoes (page 98)

4 dried cloves of Garlic (page 82)

¼ cup dried parsley (see Herbs: Botanical, page 85)

1 tablespoon dried thyme (see Herbs: Perennial, page 87)

1. In a food processor or blender, pulse the carrots, celery, onions, bell peppers, mushrooms, tomatoes, garlic, parsley, and thyme into a smooth powder. Store in an airtight container in a cool, dark, dry spot in your pantry.

2. To use in soups, stir 2 tablespoons of the powder into 1 cup of boiling water and steep for 5 minutes before adding to soups.

PREPARATION TIP: I prefer to season soups individually with salt and pepper, but you can also add 2 tablespoons of sea salt and 1 teaspoon freshly ground black pepper to this broth powder mixture.

PER SERVING (2 TBSP) CALORIES: 5; FAT: 0G; CARBS: 1G; SUGAR: 0G; FIBER: 0G; PROTEIN: 0G; SODIUM: 6MG

Cream of Tomato Soup

YIELD 4 servings ❖ PREP TIME 5 minutes ❖ COOK TIME 20 minutes

Dried tomatoes provide a sweet, concentrated tomato flavor often absent from canned tomatoes. If you do not have dried garlic or basil, use fresh.

1 cup dried Tomatoes (page 98)

2 dried cloves of Garlic (page 82),
   ground into a fine powder

1 tablespoon dried basil
   (see Herbs: Botanical, page 85)

1 quart low-sodium vegetable
   broth, heated

¼ cup heavy (whipping) cream

Sea salt

Freshly ground black pepper

¼ cup fresh basil, cut into chiffonade

1. In a large saucepan over medium heat, stir together the tomatoes, garlic powder, dried basil, and vegetable broth. Bring to a simmer. Cook for about 20 minutes, uncovered, until the tomatoes are tender. Remove from the heat.

2. With an immersion blender, purée the soup in the pan until smooth. Let cool for a few minutes.

3. Stir in the cream. Season with sea salt and pepper.

4. To serve, top with fresh basil.

TROUBLESHOOTING: The reason you cool the soup briefly before stirring in the cream is that the higher temperature coupled with the tomatoes' acidity can curdle the cream, especially if you use a lighter dairy product such as half-and-half.

PER SERVING CALORIES: 52; FAT: 3G; CARBS: 4G; SUGAR: 1G; FIBER: 1G; PROTEIN: 3G; SODIUM: 134MG

Mint & Pea Soup

YIELD 4 servings * PREP TIME 5 minutes * COOK TIME 45 minutes to 1 hour

This soup is made almost entirely of dehydrated foods. As such, it makes a lovely packaged food gift from your kitchen. Fresh mint, in season, makes a delicious garnish. If you prefer not to use white wine, substitute 1 teaspoon of apple cider vinegar.

1 cup dried Peas (page 93)

¼ cup dried Celery (page 78)

¼ cup dried Leeks (page 90)

¼ cup dried Onions (page 92)

2 tablespoons dried mint (see Herbs: Botanical, page 85)

1 quart low-sodium vegetable broth

¼ cup dry white wine

Sea salt

Freshly ground black pepper

Fresh mint leaves (optional)

1. In a large pot over medium-low heat, stir together the peas, celery, leek, onions, dried mint, vegetable broth, and white wine. Cover and bring to a simmer. Cook for 45 to 60 minutes until the vegetables are tender.

2. If you prefer a smooth consistency, purée the soup with an immersion blender.

3. Season with sea salt and pepper. Garnish with fresh mint leaves (if using).

PER SERVING CALORIES: 115; FAT: 0G; CARBS: 18G; SUGAR: 6G; FIBER: 5G; PROTEIN: 7G; SODIUM: 98MG

Corn Chowder

YIELD 4 servings ❋ PREP TIME 5 minutes, plus 15 minutes inactive time
COOK TIME 15 minutes

This recipe is another easy and delicious soup made almost entirely of dehydrated ingredients. Don't worry if you're missing one or two of them; simply replace with fresh and double the quantity. This also makes a great food gift when packaged together—simply grind the dried corn before adding to the jar.

2 cups dried Corn (page 79), divided

½ cup dried Celery (page 78)

½ cup dried Leeks (page 90)

½ cup dried Onions (page 92)

1 teaspoon dried thyme
   (see Herbs: Perennial, page 87)

¼ teaspoon cayenne pepper

2 quarts low-sodium chicken broth
   or vegetable broth

2 tablespoons white wine vinegar

¼ cup heavy (whipping) cream

Sea salt

Freshly ground black pepper

1. In a spice grinder or food processor, pulse ½ cup of the corn kernels until smooth.

2. In a large saucepan, combine the ground corn with the remaining 1½ cups corn kernels, the celery, leeks, onions, thyme, and cayenne pepper.

3. Stir in the chicken broth and let sit for 15 minutes.

4. Over medium heat, bring to a simmer. Cook for 15 minutes, until the vegetables are tender.

5. Stir in the white wine vinegar until fully mixed.

6. Stir in the cream. Season with sea salt and pepper. If you prefer a smoother texture, purée with an immersion blender.

PREPARATION TIP: If you're preparing this soup for camping or backpacking, substitute ¼ cup of dry milk powder for the heavy cream.

PER SERVING CALORIES: 135; FAT: 3G; CARBS: 21G; SUGAR: 4G; FIBER: 3G; PROTEIN: 7G; SODIUM: 216MG

French Onion Soup

YIELD 4 servings ❊ PREP TIME 10 minutes ❊ COOK TIME 1 hour

This blend of dried vegetables and herbs is a healthy alternative to packaged onion soup mixes. It stores well and can also be used as a coating for meat or as a flavorful addition to sauces and casseroles.

1 cup thinly dried sliced Onions (page 92), divided

2 tablespoons dried diced Celery (page 78)

1 tablespoon dried parsley (see Herbs: Botanical, page 85)

1 teaspoon dried thyme (see Herbs: Perennial, page 87)

2 dried cloves of Garlic (page 82)

1 teaspoon sea salt

¼ teaspoon freshly ground black pepper

1 quart low-sodium beef broth

¼ cup dry red wine

4 slices of French bread or baguette

1 tablespoon olive oil

½ cup grated Gruyère cheese

1. In a spice grinder or food processor, combine ½ cup of the onions with the celery, parsley, thyme, and garlic. Pulse until ground to a fine powder.

2. In a large pot over low heat, add the seasoned onion powder and stir together with the remaining ½ cup onions, the sea salt, pepper, beef broth, and red wine. Cover and bring to a simmer. Cook for 30 minutes. Remove the lid and continue cooking for 30 minutes, allowing the soup to reduce and the onions to soften fully.

3. While soup is simmering, preheat oven to 450°F. Lightly brush one side of the bread slices with olive oil and place on a parchment-lined baking sheet. Place sheet in the oven and toast until lightly browned, about 5 minutes. Remove from the oven and sprinkle toast with grated cheese and return to oven. Bake until cheese is melted and lightly browned, about 5 minutes.

4. To serve, ladle soup into bowls and top each with a slice of cheesy toast bread.

PREPARATION TIP: To store this soup mix for later use, grind the onions, celery, herbs, and garlic to a powder as directed in step 1, and mix with the sea salt, pepper, and remaining sliced onions. Store in an airtight container in a cool, dark cupboard until ready to use.

PER SERVING CALORIES: 65; FAT: 0G; CARBS: 9G; SUGAR: 4G; FIBER: 2G; PROTEIN: 1G; SODIUM: 345MG

Cream of Mushroom Soup

YIELD 4 servings ❊ PREP TIME 5 minutes, plus 10 minutes inactive time
COOK TIME 25 minutes

Mushrooms are rich in umami flavor, the fifth taste that gives food a meaty, almost textural, quality found naturally in many foods. Dehydrating concentrates this effect, which makes dried mushrooms one of my favorite ingredients to use in savory cooking.

1 cup roughly chopped dried assorted Mushrooms (page 91), divided

¼ cup dried diced Celery (page 78)

¼ cup dried sliced Leeks (page 90)

¼ cup dried diced Onions (page 92)

1 quart low-sodium chicken broth or vegetable broth, heated, divided

2 tablespoons butter or extra-virgin olive oil

2 cups sliced fresh cremini mushrooms

2 tablespoons dry sherry or white wine

1 teaspoon dried thyme (see Herbs: Perennial page 87)

¼ cup heavy (whipping) cream

Sea salt

Freshly ground black pepper

1. Place half of the dried mushrooms into a spice grinder or food processor and pulse into a smooth powder.

2. Place the remaining mushrooms in a jar with the celery, leeks, and onions. Pour in enough hot chicken broth just to cover. Let sit for 10 minutes to rehydrate.

3. In a large pot over medium-high heat, melt the butter. Using a wooden spoon to stir, brown the fresh mushrooms for 1 to 2 minutes per side, in several batches, making sure not to crowd them in the pan.

4. Add the sherry to deglaze the pan, scraping up any browned bits from the bottom.

5. Add the soaked mushrooms and vegetables with their soaking liquid, the remaining chicken broth, and thyme. Reduce the heat to medium-low. Simmer for 15 to 20 minutes, uncovered, until the vegetables are soft and the soup is slightly condensed. Stir in the cream.

6. Season with sea salt and pepper.

COOKING TIP: I like to use a variety of dried mushrooms, particularly wild mushrooms. As with any recipe in this section, you can purchase and use commercially dehydrated food.

PER SERVING CALORIES: 142; FAT: 9G; CARBS: 5G; SUGAR: 2G; FIBER: 1G; PROTEIN: 4G; SODIUM: 182MG

Cream of Celery Soup

YIELD 4 servings ❖ PREP TIME 5 minutes ❖ COOK TIME 35 minutes

I love the delicate flavor of celery in this creamy, barely sweetened soup. It makes a light, delicious appetizer. For a vegan soup, use vegetable broth, and substitute coconut cream for the heavy cream.

2 cups dried diced Celery (page 78)

¼ cup dried diced Onions (page 92)

¼ cup dried sliced Leeks (page 90)

2 tablespoons dried diced Apples (page 46)

1½ quarts low-sodium chicken broth or vegetable broth

1 teaspoon white wine vinegar

¼ cup heavy (whipping) cream

Sea salt

Freshly ground black pepper

Handful of fresh celery leaves, for serving

1. In a large pot over medium-low heat, stir together the celery, onions, leeks, apples, and chicken broth. Bring to a simmer. Cover and cook for 30 minutes until the vegetables are softened.

2. Add the white wine vinegar. With an immersion blender, purée the soup until smooth.

3. Stir in the cream and cook for 5 minutes more.

4. Season with sea salt and pepper. Serve sprinkled with fresh celery leaves.

COOKING TIP: For a pretty presentation and delicious textural contrast, before garnishing, toss the fresh celery leaves with a handful of roughly chopped fresh mint and julienned Granny Smith apples.

PER SERVING CALORIES: 99; FAT: 3G; CARBS: 13G; SUGAR: 4G; FIBER: 3G; PROTEIN: 5G; SODIUM: 208MG

Minestrone Soup

YIELD 4 servings ✽ PREP TIME 5 minutes
COOK TIME 1 hour, 30 minutes to 1 hour, 45 minutes

This dried soup mix makes a beautiful food gift, especially when all the colorful ingredients are layered in a glass jar. Place the dry ingredients, minus salt and pepper, in the jar in the reverse order listed here, so the pasta is at the bottom of the jar and can be added at the end of the cooking time.

½ cup dried kidney beans

¼ cup dried diced Carrots (page 76)

¼ cup dried diced Celery (page 78)

¼ cup dried diced Onions (page 92)

2 dried cloves Garlic (page 82)

1 teaspoon dried thyme
(see Herbs: Perennial, page 87)

Pinch of red pepper flakes

2 quarts low-sodium vegetable broth

1 cup dried Tomatoes (page 98)

1 cup dried Green Beans (page 84)

Sea salt

Freshly ground black pepper

1 cup small shell pasta noodles

2 tablespoons good-quality extra-virgin
olive oil

¼ cup fresh basil, julienned

½ cup finely grated Parmesan cheese

1. In a large pot over medium-low heat, stir together the kidney beans, carrots, celery, onions, garlic, thyme, red pepper flakes, and vegetable broth. Bring to a simmer. Cover and cook for 1 hour.

2. Add the tomatoes and green beans. Continue cooking for 15 to 30 minutes, partially covered, until the beans and vegetables are nearly tender. Season with sea salt and pepper.

3. Add the pasta. Cook according to the package directions until the pasta is *al dente*.

4. Serve with a drizzle of olive oil. Sprinkle with fresh basil and Parmesan cheese.

TROUBLESHOOTING: There is some controversy about whether salt added to dried beans during cooking prevents them from softening. I have experienced this effect and avoid adding salt until the beans are nearly finished cooking.

PER SERVING CALORIES: 332; FAT: 11G; CARBS: 40G; SUGAR: 3G; FIBER: 6G; PROTEIN: 19G; SODIUM: 356MG

Broccoli-Cheddar Bisque

YIELD 4 servings * PREP TIME 5 minutes * COOK TIME 50 minutes

I prefer to use sharp Cheddar cheese in this creamy soup. Feel free to use any pungent, flavorful cheese you prefer. For a little spice, use pepper Jack cheese. Or, try a bit of smoked Cheddar for a deliciously smoky flavor. The dry ingredients in this soup can be assembled in a glass jar for a lovely food gift. Give it with a small block of sharp Cheddar cheese.

2 cups dried diced Broccoli (page 74)

¼ cup dried sliced Carrots (page 76)

¼ cup dried diced Celery (page 78)

¼ cup dried diced Onions (page 92)

2 quarts low-sodium chicken broth or vegetable broth

1 teaspoon apple cider vinegar

¼ cup heavy (whipping) cream

Sea salt

Freshly ground black pepper

1 cup grated sharp Cheddar cheese

1. In a large pot over medium-low heat, stir together the broccoli, carrots, celery, onions, and chicken broth. Bring to a simmer. Cover and cook for 45 minutes until the vegetables are softened.

2. Stir in the apple cider vinegar.

3. Transfer 2 cups of the soup to a blender and purée until very smooth. Return the puréed soup to the pot.

4. Stir in the cream and cook for 5 minutes. Season with sea salt and pepper.

5. Remove the soup from the heat and cool briefly before adding the Cheddar cheese. Stir until melted.

PER SERVING CALORIES: 220; FAT: 12G; CARBS: 13G; SUGAR: 4G; FIBER: 3G; PROTEIN: 15G; SODIUM: 403MG

Borscht

YIELD 4 servings ❖ PREP TIME 5 minutes, plus 8 hours inactive time
COOK TIME 10 to 15 minutes

Rehydrating the vegetables overnight and then simmering them for a short time in their soaking liquid allows this soup to retain more nutrients than just cooking for a long period of time. The dehydrated ingredients can be stored together for easy preparation.

1 cup dried diced Beets (page 73)

¼ cup shredded dried Cabbage (page 75)

¼ cup dried diced Celery (page 78)

¼ cup shredded dried Carrots (page 76)

¼ cup dried sliced Leeks (page 90)

1 tablespoon dried dill (see Herbs: Botanical, page 85)

¼ teaspoon ground caraway seed

1 quart low-sodium vegetable broth

1 tablespoon red wine vinegar

Sea salt

Freshly ground black pepper

1. In a large container, stir together the beets, cabbage, celery, carrots, leeks, dill, caraway seed, vegetable broth, and vinegar. Cover and refrigerate overnight.

2. Pour the rehydrated vegetables into a large pot and bring to a simmer over medium-low heat. Cook for 10 to 15 minutes until the vegetables are softened. Season with sea salt and pepper.

3. Serve hot or chill thoroughly before serving.

PER SERVING CALORIES: 91; FAT: 0G; CARBS: 18G; SUGAR: 11G; FIBER: 4G; PROTEIN: 5G; SODIUM: 65MG

Creamy Cauliflower Soup

YIELD 4 to 6 servings ✣ PREP TIME 5 minutes ✣ COOK TIME 50 minutes

Cauliflower produces a beautiful ivory-colored soup with a subtle Brassica flavor. It's delicious with garlic, thyme, and Parmesan cheese. You could also use Romanesco sauce in this recipe for a beautiful lime-colored soup. Either soup is lovely garnished with a handful of oven-roasted vegetables and a drizzle of olive oil.

2 cups dried diced Cauliflower (page 77)

¼ cup dried diced Celery (page 78)

¼ cup dried diced Onions (page 92)

2 dried cloves of Garlic (page 82)

1 sprig fresh thyme

2 quarts low-sodium chicken broth or vegetable broth

1 teaspoon white wine vinegar

¼ cup heavy (whipping) cream

Sea salt

¼ teaspoon freshly ground white pepper

¼ cup shredded Parmesan cheese

1. In a large pot over medium-low heat, stir together the cauliflower, celery, onions, garlic, thyme, and chicken broth. Bring to a simmer. Cover and cook for 45 minutes, until the vegetables are softened.

2. Remove the thyme sprig and stir in the white wine vinegar.

3. With an immersion blender, purée the soup in the pot until smooth.

4. Stir in the cream, season with sea salt, and stir in the white pepper. Cook for 5 minutes.

5. Remove the soup from the heat and cool briefly before adding the Parmesan cheese. Stir until melted.

SUBSTITUTION TIP: You can also use 1 teaspoon of dried thyme instead of the fresh thyme, but it will produce flecks in the creamy white soup.

PER SERVING CALORIES: 98; FAT: 4G; CARBS: 7G; SUGAR: 2G; FIBER: 2G; PROTEIN: 8G; SODIUM: 288MG

Kale & White Bean Soup

YIELD 4 servings * PREP TIME 5 minutes * COOK TIME 30 to 40 minutes

This soup makes dinner preparation a cinch. For a more filling and meaty soup, add 1 pound of cooked, crumbled Italian sausage during the last 10 minutes of cooking.

1 cup dried Kale (page 89)

½ cup dried diced Onions (page 92)

½ cup dried diced Carrots (page 77)

¼ cup dried diced Celery (page 78)

4 dried cloves Garlic (page 82)

1 cup dried halved cherry Tomatoes (page 98)

2 quarts low-sodium chicken broth or vegetable broth

1 (13-ounce) can giant white beans, rinsed and drained

1 teaspoon red wine vinegar

4 sprigs fresh dill, stems removed

Sea salt

Freshly ground black pepper

1. In a large pot over medium-low heat, stir together the kale, onions, carrots, celery, garlic, tomatoes, and chicken broth. Bring to a simmer. Cover and cook for 30 to 40 minutes until the vegetables are tender.

2. Stir in the beans, vinegar, and dill and cook until just heated through, 1 to 2 minutes.

3. Season with sea salt and pepper.

COOKING TIP: This soup can also be made in a slow cooker. Cook for 8 hours on low and add the beans about 10 minutes before the end of cooking.

PER SERVING CALORIES: 212; FAT: 1G; CARBS: 37G; SUGAR: 3G; FIBER: 13G; PROTEIN: 14G; SODIUM: 365 MG

Carrot-Ginger-Orange Soup

YIELD 2 to 4 servings ✳ PREP TIME 5 minutes, plus 8 hours inactive time
COOK TIME 15 minutes

This bright, spicy soup is a perfect starter for summer meals. With only a few minutes on the stovetop, it won't heat up your kitchen. It is also delicious served chilled with a drizzle of plain yogurt.

1 cup dried diced Carrots (page 76)

½ teaspoon dried Ginger (page 83)

½ teaspoon dried orange zest
(see Citrus Fruits, page 52)

1 quart low-sodium vegetable broth

1 teaspoon freshly squeezed lemon juice

Sea salt

Freshly ground black pepper

1. In a nonreactive container, combine the carrots, ginger, and orange zest. Stir in the vegetable broth and lemon juice. Cover and refrigerate overnight to rehydrate.

2. Pour the rehydrated vegetables into a large saucepan. Bring to a simmer over medium-low heat. Cover and cook for 15 minutes, or until the carrots are tender. Season with sea salt and pepper.

3. With an immersion blender, purée the soup. Serve.

PER SERVING CALORIES: 79; FAT: 0G; CARBS: 14G; SUGAR: 6G; FIBER: 3G; PROTEIN: 5G; SODIUM: 112MG

Leek & Potato Soup

YIELD 4 servings ❋ PREP TIME 5 minutes ❋ COOK TIME 30 to 40 minutes

Mild leeks and potatoes unite for a creamy, comforting soup. If you prefer a vegan meal, skip the butter and drizzle good-quality olive oil over the finished soup.

1 cup dried sliced Leeks (page 90)

1 cup dried diced Potatoes (page 95)

¼ cup dried diced Celery (page 78)

2 dried cloves of Garlic (page 82)

1 teaspoon dried thyme
  (see Herbs: Perennial, page 87)

2 quarts low-sodium chicken broth
  or vegetable broth

¼ cup dry white wine

2 tablespoons butter

Sea salt

Freshly ground black pepper

1. In a large pot over medium-low heat, stir together the leeks, potatoes, celery, garlic, thyme, chicken broth, and white wine. Bring to a simmer. Cover and cook for 30 to 40 minutes until the vegetables are tender.

2. Transfer 1 cup of soup to a blender. Add the butter. Purée until very smooth. Return the puréed soup to the pot and stir to mix. Season with sea salt and pepper.

PER SERVING CALORIES: 147; FAT: 6G; CARBS: 20G; SUGAR: 4G; FIBER: 2G; PROTEIN: 2G; SODIUM: 124MG

Vegetarian & Vegan Entrées

Ratatouille 186

Root Vegetable
Gratin 187

Mushroom & Pea
Risotto 188

Polenta with
Mushrooms 190

Spicy Veggie Chickpea
Burgers 192

Vegetarian Fried
Rice 194

Spicy Thai Curry 195

Loaded Sweet Potato
Tacos 196

Corn Fritters 197

Eggplant, Zucchini, &
Spinach Lasagna 198

Mushroom & Tomato
Frittata 200

Zucchini-Oregano-
Lemon Frittata 201

Ratatouille

YIELD 4 servings ❊ PREP TIME 5 minutes ❊ COOK TIME 1 hour, 15 minutes

The ingredients for this vegetable stew are bountiful at summer's end. And the flavor and texture of this dish are particularly wonderful in the dead of winter—so warm and comforting! Make sure to keep some dehydrated zucchini, eggplant, and tomatoes in your pantry for when the weather turns cold. Serve with a glass of Syrah and crusty whole-grain bread.

1 tablespoon extra-virgin olive oil

1 cup dried sliced Zucchini (page 99)

1 cup dried sliced Tomatoes (page 98)

1 cup dried sliced Eggplant (page 81)

½ cup dried sliced Onions (page 92)

2 dried cloves of Garlic (page 82),
  ground to a fine powder

1 teaspoon dried thyme
  (see Herbs: Perennial, page 87)

Sea salt

Freshly ground black pepper

6 cups low-sodium vegetable broth

1. Preheat the oven to 325°F.

2. Coat the interior of a 2-quart baking dish with the olive oil.

3. Layer the zucchini, tomatoes, eggplant, and onions in the dish.

4. Sprinkle the vegetables with the garlic powder and thyme. Season with sea salt and pepper.

5. Pour in the vegetable broth, pressing the vegetables down with your hands or a wooden spoon to submerge.

6. Cover tightly with aluminum foil. Bake for 1 hour. Remove the foil and continue baking until the vegetables are soft and most of the liquid has evaporated, about 15 minutes.

PREPARATION TIP: The vegetable slices form a gratin texture. But diced vegetables also work equally well in this casserole.

PER SERVING CALORIES: 75; FAT: 4G; CARBS: 10G; SUGAR: 5G; FIBER: 4G; PROTEIN: 3G; SODIUM: 101MG

Root Vegetable Gratin

YIELD 4 servings   ❋   PREP TIME 10 minutes   ❋   COOK TIME 1 hour, 17 minutes

Potatoes are the most common vegetable for a gratin in American cooking. This version uses assorted root vegetables and is lighter than most gratins in that it's not cooked in a béchamel sauce. But the toasted bread crumbs and Parmesan cheese that top the dish add a decadent finish.

1 tablespoon extra-virgin olive oil

2 cups dried Root Vegetables (page 96)

2 dried cloves of Garlic (page 82), ground to a fine powder

1 teaspoon minced dried rosemary (see Herbs: Perennial, page 87)

¼ teaspoon sea salt

Freshly ground black pepper

1 quart low-sodium vegetable broth

¼ cup panko bread crumbs

¼ cup grated Parmesan cheese

1. Preheat the oven to 350°F.

2. Coat the interior of a 2-quart casserole dish with the olive oil.

3. Spread the root vegetables in the dish.

4. Season with the garlic powder, rosemary, sea salt, and pepper.

5. Pour in the vegetable broth, pressing down on the vegetables with your hands or a wooden spoon to submerge.

6. Cover the dish tightly with aluminum foil. Bake for 1 hour. Remove the foil and continue baking until the vegetables are tender and the moisture is mostly evaporated, about 15 minutes. Remove from the oven.

7. Preheat the broiler.

8. Over the casserole, sprinkle the panko and Parmesan cheese. Place the dish on the top oven rack and broil until the bread crumbs are lightly browned and the cheese melts, 1 to 2 minutes, watching carefully so it doesn't burn.

COOKING TIP: Use parsnips, sweet potatoes, and turnips in this gratin.

PER SERVING CALORIES: 104; FAT: 6G; CARBS: 11G; SUGAR: 2G; FIBER: 2G; PROTEIN: 4G; SODIUM: 236MG

Mushroom & Pea Risotto

YIELD 2 to 4 servings ❋ PREP TIME 10 minutes ❋ COOK TIME 30 to 45 minutes

Mushroom powder has so many uses, and this creamy, vegan risotto is one of my favorites. The recipe is adapted from a recipe by one of my favorite chefs, Tyler Florence. He suggests stirring in good-quality Parmesan cheese, which is delicious. This dairy-free version is lighter and still delicious.

½ cup dried Peas (page 93)

3 cups boiling water

1 cup dried sliced Mushrooms
(page 91), divided

2 dried cloves of Garlic (page 82)

2 tablespoons extra-virgin olive oil

1 cup arborio rice or other
short-grain rice

¼ cup dried diced Onions (page 92)

1 teaspoon dried thyme
(see Herbs: Perennial, page 87)

½ teaspoon dried lemon zest
(see Citrus Fruits, page 52)

Sea salt

Freshly ground black pepper

¼ cup dry white wine

1 quart low-sodium vegetable
broth, heated

1 lemon, cut into wedges

¼ cup roughly chopped
fresh parsley

1. In a heatproof container, cover the peas with 2 cups of the boiling water. Cover and set aside to rehydrate for 30 to 45 minutes while you prepare the other ingredients and begin cooking the risotto.

2. In a separate heatproof container, combine ½ cup of the mushrooms with the remaining 1 cup boiling water and set aside to rehydrate.

3. In a spice grinder, grind the remaining ½ cup mushrooms and the garlic into a fine powder.

4. In a large skillet over medium heat, heat the olive oil. Add the rice and stir to coat thoroughly with the oil, 1 to 2 minutes.

5. Add the mushroom and garlic powder, onions, thyme, and lemon zest and stir. Season with sea salt and pepper. Cook for 1 to 2 minutes.

6. Pour in the white wine and cook for about 2 minutes until it is mostly absorbed.

7. Pour in 1 cup of the heated vegetable broth, stirring constantly. When the mixture is nearly absorbed, add another cup of vegetable broth. Continue cooking and stirring until the liquid is absorbed.

8. Drain the mushrooms, reserving the mushroom broth. Strain the mushroom broth to remove any sediment. Stir in the mushrooms and their strained broth.

9. Drain the peas. Add them to the pan. Continue cooking and stirring until the mushroom broth is absorbed.

10. Add more vegetable broth, cook, and stir until the rice is al dente, the peas are soft, and nearly all the vegetable broth is absorbed.

11. Serve with the lemon wedges and garnish with the fresh parsley.

COOKING TIP: Don't rush the risotto. It takes time for the rice to cook and release its starch.

PER SERVING CALORIES: 536; FAT: 14G; CARBS: 86G; SUGAR: 6G; FIBER: 4G; PROTEIN: 10G; SODIUM: 130MG

Polenta with Mushrooms

YIELD 2 to 4 servings ✱ PREP TIME 10 minutes ✱ COOK TIME 15 to 20 minutes

I love one-pot meals, especially in my small apartment kitchen, and this one is worth the extra attention. The butter added to the mushrooms at the end is a classic French cooking technique and brings an extra bit of flavor to the meal.

1 cup dried sliced Mushrooms (page 91)

1 cup hot water

3 cups low-sodium vegetable broth

1 cup dried Corn (page 79), coarsely ground

¼ cup grated Parmesan cheese

1 tablespoon extra-virgin olive oil

1 tablespoon dried Onions (page 92), ground to a fine powder

1 teaspoon dried thyme (see Herbs: Perennial, page 87)

1 dried clove of Garlic (page 82), ground to a fine powder

1 tablespoon dry sherry or white wine

1 tablespoon cold butter

Sea salt

Freshly ground black pepper

1. In a heatproof container, combine the mushrooms and hot water. Set aside to rehydrate for 10 minutes.

2. In a large saucepan over medium-low heat, bring the vegetable broth to a simmer. Slowly pour in the ground corn, stirring constantly. Cook for about 15 minutes until the mixture thickens and the corn becomes tender.

3. Stir in the Parmesan cheese. Turn off the heat but keep warm.

4. While the polenta cooks, drain the mushrooms and reserve the mushroom broth. Strain the mushroom broth to remove any sediment and set aside.

5. In a large skillet over medium heat, heat the olive oil. Add the drained mushrooms to the skillet.

6. Stir in the onion powder, thyme, and garlic powder. Cook for 5 minutes.

7. Add the sherry and ¼ cup of the strained mushroom broth. Season with sea salt and pepper. Continue cooking for about 5 minutes, or until all the liquid has evaporated.

8. Remove the pan from the heat and whisk in the cold butter to finish the sauce.

9. Divide the polenta between serving bowls and top with the mushrooms.

SUBSTITUTION TIP: I usually keep a bottle of dry sherry and white wine in my refrigerator for cooking. But if you don't have either, or prefer to cook without alcohol, use 1 teaspoon of white wine vinegar and 2 teaspoons of the strained mushroom broth.

PER SERVING CALORIES: 232; FAT: 17G; CARBS: 18G; SUGAR: 3G; FIBER: 2G; PROTEIN: 8G; SODIUM: 293MG

Spicy Veggie Chickpea Burgers

YIELD 4 servings ❖ PREP TIME 15 minutes ❖ COOK TIME 10 minutes

Making your own veggie burgers saves money and spares you a long list of processed ingredients present in most commercial veggie burgers. These get a gentle kick from cayenne pepper, but you could certainly bump up the spice with additional cayenne pepper or red pepper flakes.

1 cup cooked chickpeas

2 tablespoons dried diced Onions (page 92)

2 tablespoons dried diced bell Peppers (page 94)

1 dried clove of Garlic (page 82), ground to a fine powder

1 teaspoon ground cumin

1 teaspoon smoked paprika

¼ teaspoon ground cayenne pepper

¼ teaspoon sea salt

1 egg, beaten

½ cup panko bread crumbs

2 tablespoons canola oil

1. Combine the chickpeas, onions, bell peppers, garlic powder, cumin, paprika, cayenne pepper, and sea salt in a food processor or blender.

2. Pulse until the chickpeas are gently mashed and the spices are blended in. Allow the mixture to rest for at least 10 minutes.

3. Stir or blend in the egg and bread crumbs.

4. Form the chickpea mixture into 4 patties. Allow to rest for another 10 minutes to help the ingredients set.

5. Heat the oil in a large skillet over medium heat. Cook the burgers for 5 to 7 minutes, or until browned. Flip and cook for another 5 to 7 minutes.

6. Serve alone or with traditional burger buns, lettuce, tomatoes, and condiments.

SUBSTITUTION TIP: To keep these burgers gluten-free, look for gluten-free bread crumbs online, or make your own by gently toasting cubes of gluten-free bread and then grinding into crumbs.

PER SERVING (1 BURGER) CALORIES: 217; FAT: 11G; CARBS: 23G; SUGAR: 2G; FIBER: 4G; PROTEIN: 8G; SODIUM: 240MG

Vegetarian Fried Rice

YIELD 2 to 4 servings ❋ PREP TIME 5 minutes, plus 1 hour inactive time
COOK TIME 10 minutes

Day-old cooked rice works best for making fried rice, which is fortunate because it's not very useful for much else. This vegetarian version omits the Chinese sausage that is often present in fried rice.

¼ cup dried Peas (page 93)

¼ cup dried diced Carrots (page 76)

2 cups hot water

2 tablespoons peanut oil

2 large eggs, beaten

2 scallions, white and light green parts only, thinly sliced, separated

2 cups cooked cooled rice, brown or white

1 teaspoon dried Ginger (page 83), ground to a fine powder

1 dried clove of Garlic (page 82), ground to a fine powder

1 tablespoon soy sauce

1 teaspoon rice wine vinegar

Sea salt

Freshly ground black pepper

1. In a heatproof container, combine the peas, carrots, and hot water. Set aside to rehydrate for 1 hour.

2. In a large skillet over medium heat, heat the peanut oil. Pour in the eggs and cook, undisturbed, for 1 minute. Carefully flip and cook the other side for about 30 seconds, or until cooked through. Transfer to a cutting board and slice into thin ribbons.

3. In the same skillet, add the white parts of the scallions, the rice, ginger, and garlic powder. Cook for 2 to 3 minutes.

4. Drain the peas and carrots and add them to the skillet.

5. Stir in the soy sauce and rice wine vinegar. Cook for 3 to 4 minutes until the vegetables are heated through.

6. Season with sea salt and pepper before serving. Garnish with light green scallions.

PREPARATION TIP: *To make this dish a main course, use 4 eggs and garnish with toasted slivered almonds.*

PER SERVING CALORIES: 238; FAT: 10G; CARBS: 31G; SUGAR: 2G; FIBER: 2G; PROTEIN: 7G; SODIUM: 331MG

Spicy Thai Curry

YIELD 4 servings ❋ PREP TIME 5 minutes, plus 30 minutes inactive time
COOK TIME 20 minutes

The sweet and spicy flavors of red curry liven up everyday vegetables. Feel free to increase the amount of curry or swap it for green or yellow curry paste for a change of pace. Serve with rice or rice noodles. For a low-carb option, serve over zucchini noodles.

1 cup dried diced Eggplant (page 81)

1 cup dried sliced green bell Peppers (page 94)

½ cup dried sliced Onions (page 92)

4 cups hot water

1 (15-ounce) can full-fat coconut milk

1 tablespoon low-sodium soy sauce

¼ cup dried diced Pineapple (page 65)

1 tablespoon red curry paste

1 teaspoon dried Ginger (page 83), ground to a fine powder

1 dried clove of Garlic (page 82), ground to a fine powder

1 tablespoon freshly squeezed lime juice

1 teaspoon honey or agave nectar

Sea salt

Freshly ground black pepper

1. In a heatproof container, combine the eggplant, peppers, onions, and hot water. Set aside to rehydrate for 30 minutes. Drain, reserving 1 cup soaking liquid.

2. In a large saucepan over medium-low heat, stir together the rehydrated vegetables and the reserved soaking liquid.

3. Add the coconut milk, soy sauce, pineapple, red curry paste, ground ginger, and garlic powder and stir to combine. Bring to a simmer. Cover and cook for about 20 minutes until the vegetables are tender.

4. Stir in the lime juice and honey. Season with sea salt and pepper.

5. Divide curry among bowls and top with fresh herbs like cilantro or basil (optional).

INGREDIENT TIP: For more protein, drain and press 16 ounces of tofu, and cut into ½-inch dice. Add to the curry about 5 minutes before stirring in the lime juice and honey.

PER SERVING CALORIES: 302; FAT: 27G; CARBS: 17G; SUGAR: 10G; FIBER: 5G; PROTEIN: 4G; SODIUM: 435MG

Loaded Sweet Potato Tacos

YIELD 4 servings ❖ PREP TIME 10 minutes, plus 1 hour inactive time
COOK TIME 30 minutes

Onions, peppers, and sweet potatoes build a delicious base of flavor in these vegetarian tacos. With a dollop of guacamole, pico de gallo, and sour cream, they make a delicious entrée.

1 cup diced Sweet Potatoes
   (see Root Vegetables, page 96)

½ cup dried diced Onions (page 92)

½ cup dried diced bell Peppers
   (page 94), any color

3 cups hot water

2 tablespoons canola oil

8 ounces tempeh, crumbled

2 dried cloves of Garlic (page 82), ground
   to a fine powder

1 teaspoon ground cumin

1 teaspoon smoked paprika

2 tablespoons ketchup

Sea salt

Freshly ground black pepper

8 hard-shell corn tortillas

½ cup pico de gallo

¼ cup prepared guacamole

¼ cup sour cream

1 cup shredded lettuce

1. In a heatproof container, combine the sweet potatoes, onions, bell peppers, and hot water. Set aside for 1 hour to rehydrate. Drain.

2. In a large skillet over medium heat, heat the canola oil. Add the rehydrated vegetables. Cook, stirring often, for 20 minutes until they are soft and cooked through.

3. Add the tempeh, garlic powder, cumin, and paprika. Cook for 5 minutes.

4. Stir in the ketchup. Season with sea salt and pepper. Cook for 1 to 2 minutes.

5. Serve with the corn tortillas, pico de gallo, sour cream, and shredded lettuce.

NUTRITIONAL HIGHLIGHT: Tempeh is fermented soybeans. Many people find it easier to digest than tofu or other vegan meat alternatives.

PER SERVING CALORIES: 541; FAT: 27G; CARBS: 61G; SUGAR: 6G; FIBER: 5G; PROTEIN: 15G; SODIUM: 372MG

Corn Fritters

YIELD 24 small fritters ✽ PREP TIME 10 minutes
COOK TIME 10 minutes, plus 1 hour inactive time

My husband does not eat meat, and these corn fritters are one of his favorite appetizers. If you follow a gluten-free or grain-free diet, use tapioca flour or chickpea flour instead of wheat flour.

1 cup dried Corn (page 79)

2 tablespoons dried diced Onions (page 92)

2 tablespoons dried diced green bell Peppers (page 94)

3 cups hot water

⅓ cup all-purpose flour

1 teaspoon ground cumin

1 teaspoon ground coriander

½ teaspoon baking powder

¼ teaspoon sea salt

⅛ teaspoon ground cayenne pepper

2 tablespoons canola oil

1. In a medium heatproof bowl, combine the corn, onions, bell peppers, and hot water. Set aside to rehydrate for 1 hour.

2. In another medium bowl, mix together the flour, cumin, coriander, baking powder, sea salt, and cayenne pepper.

3. Drain the hydrated vegetables, reserving the soaking liquid. Toss the vegetables with the seasoned flour to coat. Slowly stir in ¼ cup of the soaking liquid, adding more as needed to make a sticky batter.

4. In a large skillet over medium heat, heat the canola oil. Spoon a generous scoop of batter (about 3 tablespoons for each fritter) into the pan. Fry for 3 to 4 minutes on each side, or until set.

5. Transfer the fritters to a cooling rack and repeat with the remaining batter.

SERVING SUGGESTION: A cooling dip is a delicious accompaniment to these fritters. Whisk ½ cup sour cream with 1 tablespoon mayonnaise, 1 tablespoon minced fresh mint, and 1 tablespoon minced fresh cilantro.

PER SERVING (4 FRITTERS) CALORIES: 97; FAT: 5G; CARBS: 12G; SUGAR: 1G; FIBER: 1G; PROTEIN: 2G; SODIUM: 80MG

Eggplant, Zucchini & Spinach Lasagna

YIELD 4 servings ✲ PREP TIME 10 minutes
COOK TIME 1 hour, plus 15 minutes inactive time

Vegetarian lasagna can often be too watery—but not anymore. Dehydrated vegetables soak up the tomato sauce for a firm texture and delicious flavor. This version omits regular lasagna noodles for a naturally gluten-free and low-carb meal.

32 ounces prepared marinara sauce, divided

16 ounces ricotta cheese

8 ounces grated mozzarella cheese, divided

4 ounces grated Parmesan cheese

1 egg, whisked

1 dried clove of Garlic (page 82), ground into a fine powder

1 teaspoon dried oregano (see Herbs: Perennial, page 87)

3 cups dried sliced Eggplant (page 81), divided

3 cups dried sliced Zucchini (page 99), divided

1 cup dried spinach (see Kale & Other Leafy Greens, page 89), crumbled, divided

1 cup roughly chopped fresh basil, divided

1. Preheat the oven to 350°F.

2. In a 9-by-13-inch baking dish, spread $\frac{1}{2}$ cup of the marinara sauce over the bottom.

3. In a medium bowl, stir together the ricotta, 4 ounces of the mozzarella, the Parmesan, egg, garlic powder, and oregano.

4. Using about 1 cup each of the eggplant and zucchini in the baking dish, make the first layer, alternating the vegetables as you lay them flat.

5. Make a second layer with about one-third of the remaining marinara sauce.

6. Make a third layer with about one-third of the ricotta mixture.

7. Top with about $\frac{1}{3}$ cup of the spinach and $\frac{1}{3}$ cup of the fresh basil.

8. Repeat the layers until all the ingredients have been used, finishing with spinach and basil.

9. Cover the baking dish tightly with aluminum foil. Bake for 45 minutes. Remove from the oven, remove the foil, and top the casserole with the remaining 4 ounces mozzarella. Return to the oven and bake until the cheese in lightly browned and bubbling, about 15 minutes.

10. Let rest for 10 to 15 minutes before cutting and serving.

SUBSTITUTION TIP: You can replace the mozzarella and Parmesan cheeses with your favorite Italian cheese blend. Cottage cheese also works well in place of the ricotta, though it has a more pronounced flavor.

PER SERVING CALORIES: 674; FAT: 33G; CARBS: 51G; SUGAR: 26G; FIBER: 12G; PROTEIN: 47G; SODIUM: 1719MG

Mushroom & Tomato Frittata

YIELD 2 servings ❧ PREP TIME 5 minutes, plus 1 hour inactive time
COOK TIME 20 minutes

The simplicity of a frittata makes it a perfect weeknight supper. Get a head start on dinner by rehydrating the vegetables in the morning. This dish pairs well with a light side salad and crusty bread.

½ cup dried sliced Mushrooms
   (page 91)

½ cup dried sliced Tomatoes (page 98)

2 tablespoons dried diced Onions
   (page 92)

2 cups low-sodium vegetable broth
   or water, heated

5 large eggs

1 teaspoon dried thyme
   (see Herbs: Perennial, page 87)

1 dried clove of Garlic (page 82),
   ground to a fine powder

Sea salt

Freshly ground black pepper

1 tablespoon butter or extra-virgin
   olive oil

1. In a heatproof container, combine the mushrooms, tomatoes, onions, and vegetable broth. Set aside to rehydrate for 1 hour. Alternatively, use cold broth or water and rehydrate in the refrigerator for at least 2 hours and up to 8 hours.

2. Preheat the oven to 325°F.

3. Drain the vegetables, squeezing out the excess water.

4. In a medium bowl, beat the eggs, thyme, and garlic powder to combine. Season with sea salt and pepper.

5. In a medium ovenproof skillet over medium-high heat, melt the butter. Add the drained vegetables and sauté for 3 to 4 minutes.

6. Pour in the eggs. Cook for 3 to 4 minutes, allowing the eggs to brown gently around the edges.

7. Bake for 10 minutes, or until the eggs are set.

8. Carefully remove from the oven. Slice into wedges and serve.

NUTRITIONAL HIGHLIGHT: Rehydrating vegetables in cold liquid preserves more of their nutrients.

PER SERVING CALORIES: 276; FAT: 19G; CARBS: 11G; SUGAR: 7G; FIBER: 2G; PROTEIN: 19G; SODIUM: 618MG

Zucchini-Oregano-Lemon Frittata

YIELD 2 servings ✳ PREP TIME 5 minutes, plus 30 minutes inactive time
COOK TIME 20 minutes

This frittata, with hints of the Mediterranean, is rich and flavorful. If you have sliced or shredded zucchini, it can also be used. Extra-virgin olive oil has a lower smoking point than butter, so I prefer to use butter or coconut oil. For a dairy-free version, use vegetable oil and omit the feta cheese.

1 cup dried diced Zucchini (page 99)

2 cups low-sodium vegetable broth
or water

4 large eggs

1 teaspoon dried thyme
(see Herbs: Perennial, page 87)

1 teaspoon dried oregano
(see Herbs: Perennial, page 87)

½ teaspoon dried lemon zest
(see Citrus Fruits, page 52)

1 dried clove of Garlic (page 82),
ground to a fine powder

Sea salt

Freshly ground black pepper

1 tablespoon butter or extra-virgin olive oil

¼ cup feta cheese

1. In a heatproof container, combine the zucchini and vegetable broth. Set aside to rehydrate for 30 minutes. Alternatively, use cold broth and rehydrate in the refrigerator for at least 1 hour and up to 8 hours.

2. Preheat the oven to 325°F.

3. Drain the zucchini, squeezing out the excess moisture.

4. In a medium bowl, whisk the eggs, thyme, oregano, lemon zest, and garlic powder. Season with sea salt and pepper.

5. In a medium ovenproof skillet over medium-high heat, melt the butter. Add the zucchini and sauté for 3 to 4 minutes.

6. Pour in the eggs. Cook for 3 to 4 minutes, allowing the eggs to brown gently around the edges.

7. Place skillet in the oven and bake for 10 minutes, or until the eggs are set.

8. Carefully remove the hot skillet from the oven. Slice into wedges and serve.

PER SERVING CALORIES: 269; FAT: 19G; CARBS: 9G; SUGAR: 5G; FIBER: 3G; PROTEIN: 17G; SODIUM: 476MG

Meat & Poultry Entrées

Apricot Chicken with Rosemary 204

Sweet Potato Chicken Nachos 205

Southwestern Stuffed Chicken Breasts 206

Chicken Skewers Agrodolce with Dried Figs 217

Lamb Meatballs with Tzatziki Sauce 208

Spanish Lamb Stew 210

Pan-Seared Pork Chops with Mango Chutney 211

Sweet-&-Sour Meatballs with Pineapple 212

Herb-Crusted Pork Loin with Cranberry Sauce 214

Pork Tenderloin with Stewed Pears 216

Hearty Beef Chili 217

Shepherd's Pie 218

Cabbage & Beef Stew 220

Mushroom & Rosemary–Crusted Beef Tenderloin 221

Meatballs with Italian Herbed Marinara 222

Apricot Chicken with Rosemary

YIELD 2 servings ✻ PREP TIME 5 minutes ✻ COOK TIME 40 minutes

Rosemary and fruit are one of my favorite flavor combinations. In this sweet and savory dish, they liven up chicken breasts. Serve with mashed potatoes, or steamed asparagus for a low-carb option.

1 tablespoon dried rosemary
   (see Herbs: Perennial, page 87)

1 dried clove of Garlic (page 82)

¼ teaspoon sea salt

⅛ teaspoon red pepper flakes

2 (6- to 8-ounce) boneless, skinless
   chicken breasts, patted dry

2 tablespoons extra-virgin olive oil

1 shallot, minced

¼ cup dry white wine

1 cup low-sodium chicken broth

½ cup dried Apricots (page 47)

1. Preheat the oven to 350°F.

2. In a spice grinder or a mortar and pestle, coarsely grind the rosemary, garlic, sea salt, and red pepper flakes.

3. Season the chicken on all sides with the spice mixture.

4. In a medium ovenproof skillet over medium heat, heat the olive oil. Add the chicken and brown for 3 to 4 minutes on each side. Transfer to a plate.

5. Add the shallots to the skillet. Cook for about 2 minutes, stirring often with a wooden spoon, until barely softened.

6. Add the white wine to deglaze the pan, scraping up any browned bits from the bottom.

7. Stir in the chicken broth and apricots.

8. Return the chicken to the skillet. Place skillet in the oven and bake for about 30 minutes until the chicken is cooked through (to an internal temperature of 165°F).

COOKING TIP: To help keep the chicken tender throughout the cooking process, consider using bone-in chicken breasts with the skin removed.

PER SERVING CALORIES: 555; FAT: 29G; CARBS: 7G; SUGAR: 4G; FIBER: 2G; PROTEIN: 59G; SODIUM: 332MG

Sweet Potato Chicken Nachos

YIELD 2 servings ❖ PREP TIME 5 minutes ❖ COOK TIME 35 to 40 minutes

These aren't really nachos in the traditional fried-corn-chips-smothered-in-cheese sort of way. But they are exploding with flavor and one of my absolute favorite dinners. Be sure to use dehydrated sweet potatoes that have been blanched for an extra 3 to 4 minutes so they are snappy little chips.

½ cup dried sliced Tomatoes (page 98)

¼ cup dried diced Onions (page 92)

2 tablespoons dried Dates (page 55)

1 dried clove of Garlic (page 82)

1 quart low-sodium chicken broth

1 teaspoon smoked paprika

1 teaspoon ground cumin

1 teaspoon Dijon mustard

1 tablespoon apple cider vinegar

2 (6- to 8-ounce) boneless, skinless chicken breasts

2 tablespoons freshly squeezed lime juice

1 tablespoon mayonnaise

1 cup shredded fresh cabbage

2 cups dried sliced Sweet Potatoes (see Root Vegetables, page 96)

1. In a medium saucepan over medium-low heat, stir together the tomatoes, onions, dates, garlic, and chicken broth. Bring to a simmer. Cover and cook for 15 to 20 minutes until the tomatoes are tender. With an immersion blender, purée until smooth.

2. Stir in the paprika, cumin, mustard, and apple cider vinegar.

3. Add the chicken breasts. Cover and simmer for 20 minutes until the chicken is cooked through (to an internal temperature of 165°F). Transfer the chicken to a cutting board and shred with two forks. Return to the pan and stir into the sauce. Cover and turn off the heat.

4. Just before serving, in a medium bowl, stir together the lime juice and mayonnaise. Add the cabbage and toss to coat with the dressing.

5. To serve, top the dried sweet potato chips with the chicken and sauce. Garnish with the cabbage slaw.

PREPARATION TIP: I prefer the airy texture and beautiful green hue of Savoy cabbage, but use any fresh cabbage you like.

PER SERVING CALORIES: 684; FAT: 16G; CARBS: 78G; SUGAR: 12G; FIBER: 13G; PROTEIN: 55G; SODIUM: 259MG

Southwestern Stuffed Chicken Breasts

YIELD 4 servings ❊ PREP TIME 20 minutes
COOK TIME 50 minutes, plus 15 minutes inactive time

The inspiration for this dish comes from one I enjoyed at a restaurant in Phoenix. It was so scrumptious I still think of it, five years later. This version is pretty close to the original and uses ingredients you probably have in your pantry, especially if you had your dehydrator humming at the end of summer when corn and tomatoes were in season.

½ cup dried Corn (page 79)

½ cup dried sliced Tomatoes (page 98)

¼ cup dried diced Onions (page 92)

2 dried cloves of Garlic (page 82),
    ground to a fine powder

2 cups low-sodium vegetable broth

½ cup crumbled goat cheese

1 teaspoon ground coriander

¼ teaspoon cayenne pepper

1 teaspoon canola oil

4 (6- to 8-ounce) boneless, skinless
    chicken breasts

¼ teaspoon sea salt

¼ cup roughly chopped fresh cilantro

1. In a medium bowl, combine the corn, tomatoes, onions, garlic powder, and vegetable broth. Rehydrate for 15 minutes. Drain the vegetables (will still be somewhat stiff), squeezing out the excess moisture. Return to the bowl.

2. Stir in the goat cheese, coriander, and cayenne pepper.

3. Preheat the oven to 350°F.

4. Lightly grease a large baking dish with canola oil.

5. On a cutting board, slice the chicken breasts in half lengthwise almost all the way through, but not completely, so the breasts open like a book.

6. Divide the vegetable and goat cheese mixture among the 4 chicken breasts. Close the chicken breasts up over the filling and place them in the prepared baking dish. Cover the baking dish tightly with aluminum foil.

7. Bake for 40 minutes. Remove the foil and continue baking until the chicken is cooked through (to an internal temperature of 165°F) and the filling is hot, about 10 minutes.

PER SERVING CALORIES: 423; FAT: 19G; CARBS: 6G; SUGAR: 2G; FIBER: 1G; PROTEIN: 54G; SODIUM: 315MG

Chicken Skewers Agrodolce with Dried Figs

Yield 4 servings ❖ PREP TIME 15 minutes, plus 1 hour inactive time
COOK TIME 25 minutes

This recipe is delicious prepared on an outdoor grill, but a grill pan on the stovetop will work as well. Serve over couscous or quinoa for a complete meal. Agrodolce adds a sweet-sour flavor and is optional, but worth the extra effort!

2 cups dried halved Figs (page 56)

4 cups water

2 tablespoons honey

¼ cup white wine vinegar

2 pounds boneless, skinless chicken breasts, cut into 1 to 2 inch cubes

Olive oil

Sea salt

Freshly ground pepper

4 lemons, halved

½ cup loosely packed fresh parsley, for garnish

1. Soak the figs in cold water for 1 hour. They should still be slightly firm. Drain and reserve the soaking water.

2. To prepare the agrodulce, pour the fig-soaking water into a small saucepan and add the honey and vinegar. Bring to a gentle simmer over medium-low heat, stirring often, and reduce until thick and syrupy, about 15 minutes. Remove from the heat.

3. Meanwhile, thread the chicken and figs onto bamboo skewers. Brush with olive oil and season generously with salt and pepper.

4. Preheat an outdoor grill or grill pan to medium heat. Place the lemon halves cut-side down on the grill. Grill the skewers for about 10 to 15 minutes, turning occasionally, until the chicken is cooked through.

5. Place the cooked skewers on a serving platter and drizzle with the agrodolce and sprinkle with fresh parsley. Serve the lemon halves on the side.

SUBSTITUTION TIP: If you do not have honey, use another sweetener such as maple syrup, agave syrup, or brown sugar.

PER SERVING CALORIES: 727; FAT: 19G; CARBS: 73G; SUGAR: 56G; FIBER: 10G; PROTEIN: 69G; SODIUM: 269MG

Lamb Meatballs with Tzatziki Sauce

YIELD 4 servings ❖ PREP TIME 15 minutes, plus 30 minutes inactive time
COOK TIME 10 minutes

Lamb meatballs are delicious in whole-grain pita pockets or served over dressed, mixed greens and drizzled with tangy tzatziki sauce.

FOR THE TZATZIKI SAUCE

1 cup plain yogurt

½ cup dried diced Cucumber (page 80)

1 teaspoon dried dill
(see Herbs: Botanical, page 85)

1 teaspoon dried lemon zest
(see Citrus Fruits, page 52)

1 dried clove of Garlic (page 82),
ground to a fine powder

⅛ teaspoon sea salt

FOR THE MEATBALLS

1 pound lean ground lamb

1 egg, beaten

¼ cup bread crumbs

¼ cup dried diced Onions (page 92)

1 dried clove of Garlic (page 82),
ground to a fine powder

½ teaspoon dried rosemary
(see Herbs: Perennial, page 87)

⅛ teaspoon sea salt

Freshly ground black pepper

2 tablespoons extra-virgin olive oil

To make the tzatziki sauce

In a small bowl, whisk the yogurt, cucumber, dill, lemon zest, garlic powder, and sea salt. Refrigerate for about 40 minutes to allow the cucumbers to soften while preparing the meatballs.

To make the meatballs

1. In a medium bowl, mix the lamb, egg, bread crumbs, onions, garlic powder, rosemary, and sea salt. Season with pepper.

2. Form the mixture into balls about the size of golf balls. Set them on a tray and refrigerate for at least 30 minutes or up to overnight to allow the flavors to blend and the onions to soften.

3. In a large skillet over medium heat, heat the olive oil. Add the meatballs and cook for about 10 minutes, turning carefully to brown on all sides, until cooked through (to an internal temperature of 160°F).

4. Serve with the tzatziki sauce.

PER SERVING CALORIES: 375; FAT: 18G; CARBS: 14G; SUGAR: 6G; FIBER: 1G; PROTEIN: 38G; SODIUM: 314MG

Spanish Lamb Stew

YIELD 4 servings ❖ PREP TIME 10 minutes ❖ COOK TIME 1 hour 45 minutes

The dry ingredients in this lamb stew are perfect for mixing and storing in a jar until you're ready to make this dish. It makes preparation a breeze! Serve this stew on its own or over steamed long-grain rice to soak up all the delicious juices.

1 tablespoon coconut oil

1 pound lamb stew meat, cut into
   1-inch cubes

Sea salt

Freshly ground black pepper

1 cup dry red wine

1 (15-ounce) can cannellini beans,
   rinsed and drained

1 cup dried sliced Onions (page 92)

1 cup dried sliced bell Peppers,
   any color (page 94)

½ cup dried sliced Tomatoes (page 98)

2 dried cloves of Garlic (page 82)

1 tablespoon dried parsley
   (see Herbs: Botanical, page 85)

1 teaspoon dried rosemary
   (see Herbs: Perennial, page 87)

1 teaspoon smoked paprika

¼ teaspoon cayenne pepper

1 quart low-sodium beef broth

1 tablespoon sherry vinegar

1. In a large pot over medium-high heat, heat the coconut oil.

2. Pat the lamb cubes dry with paper towels. Season with sea salt and pepper. Add them to the pot and brown for 1 to 2 minutes on each side. You may have to do this in batches so as not to crowd the pan.

3. Add the red wine to deglaze the pan, scraping up any browned bits from the bottom with a wooden spoon.

4. Add the beans, onions, bell peppers, tomatoes, garlic, parsley, rosemary, paprika, and cayenne pepper.

5. Stir in the beef broth and sherry vinegar. Bring to a simmer. Reduce the heat to low. Cover and cook for 1½ hours until the lamb and vegetables are very tender. Divide among bowls and serve immediately.

COOKING TIP: For even easier prep, brown the meat on the stovetop, and then transfer it to a slow cooker and cook for 8 hours on low.

PER SERVING CALORIES: 418; FAT: 13G; CARBS: 26G; SUGAR: 7G; FIBER: 8G; PROTEIN: 39G; SODIUM: 428MG

Pan-Seared Pork Chops with Mango Chutney

YIELD 4 servings ❖ PREP TIME 10 minutes ❖ COOK TIME 20 minutes

I love the flavors of Indian curry powder and sweet mangos in this tangy sauce. It is also delicious with grilled chicken. Serve this dish with steamed vegetables or a side salad.

FOR THE CHUTNEY

1 cup dried diced Mango (page 59)

½ cup dried diced Pineapple (page 65)

¼ cup dried diced red Onions (page 92)

2 tablespoons dried sliced Tomatoes (page 98), ground to a fine powder

1 tablespoon Indian curry powder

1 dried clove of Garlic (page 82), ground to a fine powder

Pinch of red pepper flakes

1½ cups low-sodium chicken broth

¼ cup apple cider vinegar

FOR THE PORK CHOPS

4 (6-ounce) pork chops

Sea salt

Freshly ground black pepper

1 tablespoon coconut oil

To make the mango chutney

1. In a medium saucepan over medium heat, mix the mango, pineapple, onions, tomato powder, Indian curry powder, garlic powder, and red pepper flakes.

2. Stir in the chicken broth and apple cider vinegar. Bring to a simmer. Cook for about 20 minutes, stirring often, until the fruit is tender and fragrant and the sauce is thick.

To make the pork chops

1. While the chutney cooks, season the pork chops with sea salt and pepper.

2. In a large skillet over medium heat, heat the coconut oil. Sear the chops for 5 to 7 minutes per side until the interior is no longer bright pink and they've reached a minimum internal temperature of 145°F.

3. Serve the pork chops with the mango chutney.

PREPARATION TIP: Store the dried ingredients and spices for the chutney together in a jar so you're ready to make this yummy condiment at a moment's notice.

PER SERVING CALORIES: 626; FAT: 46G; CARBS: 12G; SUGAR: 9G; FIBER: 2G; PROTEIN: 39G; SODIUM: 189MG

Sweet-&-Sour Meatballs with Pineapple

YIELD 4 servings * PREP TIME 15 minutes, plus 1 hour inactive time
COOK TIME 25 minutes

Dried pineapple brings sweetness to this sauce without any added sugar. And, the dried bell peppers and onions absorb moisture in these tasty little meatballs, meaning you can skip the traditional addition of bread crumbs.

FOR THE MEATBALLS

1 pound lean ground pork

1 egg, beaten

½ cup dried diced green bell Peppers (page 94), divided

¼ cup dried diced Onions (page 92)

⅛ teaspoon sea salt

Freshly ground black pepper

FOR THE SAUCE

2 cups low-sodium chicken broth

1 cup dried diced Pineapple (page 65)

2 tablespoons dried sliced Tomatoes (page 98), ground to a fine powder

2 tablespoons apple cider vinegar

1 tablespoon low-sodium soy sauce

1 teaspoon cornstarch

1 tablespoon water

2 tablespoons coconut oil

To make the meatballs

1. In a medium bowl, mix the pork, egg, ¼ cup of the bell peppers, the onions, and sea salt. Season with black pepper.

2. Form the mixture into balls about the size of golf balls. Set them on a tray and refrigerate for at least 1 hour or up to overnight to allow the flavors to blend and the vegetables to soften.

To make the sauce

1. While the meatballs rest, in a small saucepan over medium-low heat, stir together the chicken broth, pineapple, tomato powder, apple cider vinegar, soy sauce, and the remaining ¼ cup bell peppers. Bring to a simmer. Cook for about 15 minutes until the pineapple and peppers are tender.

2. In a small bowl, whisk the cornstarch with the water. Pour into the sauce and cook, stirring, for about 1 minute just until thickened.

To finish

1. In a large skillet over medium heat, heat the coconut oil. Add the meatballs. Cook for about 10 minutes, or until cooked through (to an internal temperature of 160°F), turning carefully to brown all sides.

2. Serve with the sauce.

PER SERVING CALORIES: 276; FAT: 12G; CARBS: 9G; SUGAR: 6G; FIBER: 1G; PROTEIN: 32G; SODIUM: 379MG

Herb-Crusted Pork Loin with Cranberry Sauce

YIELD 6 servings ✺ PREP TIME 10 minutes ✺ COOK TIME 55 minutes to 1 hour

This beautiful roast makes a delicious holiday or special-occasion meal. It's simple to make and uses several ingredients you probably have in your pantry. The apple juice does double duty by rehydrating and sweetening the cranberries, so you don't need to add sugar.

FOR THE PORK

2 dried cloves of Garlic (page 82), ground to a fine powder

1 tablespoon dried rosemary (see Herbs: Perennial, page 87)

1 tablespoon dried thyme (see Herbs: Perennial, page 87)

1 teaspoon sea salt

1 teaspoon freshly ground black pepper

1 (2-pound) boneless pork loin roast, trimmed

FOR THE CRANBERRY SAUCE

2 cups unsweetened apple juice

1 cup dried Cranberries (page 54)

1 teaspoon dried orange zest (see Citrus Fruits, page 52)

To make the pork

1. Preheat the oven to 400°F.

2. Line a baking dish with parchment paper.

3. In a small bowl, stir together the garlic powder, rosemary, thyme, sea salt, and pepper.

4. Thoroughly coat the pork roast with the herb and spice mixture. Place the pork in the prepared baking dish, fat-side down. Roast for 30 minutes.

5. Turn the pork. Roast for 25 to 30 minutes more, or until the pork is cooked through (to an internal temperature of 155°F).

To make the cranberry sauce

While the pork cooks, in a medium saucepan over medium-low heat, combine the apple juice, cranberries, and orange zest. Bring to a simmer. Cook for 20 to 30 minutes until the cranberries are soft and begin to disintegrate.

To finish

1. Let the pork rest at least 10 minutes before slicing.

2. Serve with the cranberry sauce.

TROUBLESHOOTING: If the cranberries are not sweet enough, add 1 teaspoon of honey at a time until the sauce reaches your desired level of sweetness.

PER SERVING CALORIES: 271; FAT: 6 G; CARBS: 13G; SUGAR: 10G; FIBER: 1G; PROTEIN: 40G; SODIUM: 402MG

Pork Tenderloin with Stewed Pears

YIELD 4 servings ❈ PREP TIME 10 minutes ❈ COOK TIME 30 minutes

Pork and fruit are a classic combination. I love the sweetness of the stewed pears and the added spice from the cardamom, ginger, and cinnamon. If you don't have cardamom, just omit it. The sauce will still be quite tasty.

FOR THE PEARS

2 cups dried sliced Pears (page 64)

1 teaspoon dried Ginger (page 83)

½ teaspoon ground cinnamon

¼ teaspoon ground cardamom

3½ cups water

1 tablespoon apple cider vinegar

FOR THE PORK TENDERLOIN

1 (1½-pound) pork tenderloin

1 teaspoon dried sage
   (see Herbs: Perennial, page 87)

Sea salt

Freshly ground black pepper

1 tablespoon coconut oil

To make the pears

In a medium saucepan over medium-low heat, combine the pears, ginger, cinnamon, cardamom, water, and apple cider vinegar. Bring to a simmer. Cook for 20 minutes until the pears are soft.

To make the pork tenderloin

1. Preheat the oven to 400°F.

2. While the pears cook, season the pork on all sides with the sage, sea salt, and pepper.

3. In a large ovenproof skillet over medium-high heat, heat the coconut oil. Sear the pork on all sides, for a total of about 5 minutes. Roast in the oven for 10 to 15 minutes until the pork is cooked through (to an internal temperature of 145°F). Allow the meat to rest for a few minutes before slicing.

4. Serve with the stewed pears.

SUBSTITUTION TIP: Try this recipe with a variety of dried fruits, such as figs, dates, apples, or peaches.

PER SERVING CALORIES: 342; FAT: 10G; CARBS: 18G; SUGAR: 11G; FIBER: 4G; PROTEIN: 45G; SODIUM: 163MG

Hearty Beef Chili

YIELD 4 servings ❊ PREP TIME 10 minutes ❊ COOK TIME 2 hours, 15 minutes

When I make traditional meaty chili—it's all about the vegetables! If you prefer not to cook with wine, deglaze the pan with a quarter cup of beef broth instead.

1 tablespoon coconut oil

1 pound beef chuck, cut into 1-inch cubes

Sea salt

Freshly ground black pepper

¼ cup dry red wine

½ cup dried sliced Mushrooms (page 91)

½ cup dried sliced bell Peppers, any color (page 94)

¼ cup dried diced Celery (page 78)

¼ cup dried diced Onions (page 92)

¼ cup dried diced Carrots (page 76)

¼ cup dried sliced Tomatoes (page 98), ground to a fine powder

4 dried cloves of Garlic (page 82), ground to a fine powder

1 tablespoon chili powder

1 teaspoon ground cumin

1 teaspoon smoked paprika

1 quart low-sodium beef broth

1. In a large pot over medium-high heat, heat the coconut oil.

2. Pat the beef cubes dry with paper towels. Season well with sea salt and pepper. Add them to the pan and brown for 1 to 2 minutes on each side. You may need to do this in batches so as not to crowd the pan.

3. Add the wine to deglaze the pan, using a wooden spoon to scrape up any browned bits from the bottom. Cook for 1 to 2 minutes, stirring, until the alcohol cooks off.

4. Add the mushrooms, bell peppers, celery, onions, carrots, tomato powder, garlic powder, chili powder, cumin, and paprika.

5. Stir in the beef broth until everything is combined. Cover and cook over medium-low heat for 2 hours, or until the beef is tender and the vegetables are soft. Adjust the seasonings and serve.

SUBSTITUTION TIP: If you do not have dried versions of any of these vegetables, use fresh and double the quantity. For the tomato powder, you can use 2 tablespoons of tomato paste instead.

PER SERVING CALORIES: 306; FAT: 11G; CARBS: 8G; SUGAR: 3G; FIBER: 3G; PROTEIN: 36G; SODIUM: 240MG

Shepherd's Pie

YIELD 4 servings ✢ PREP TIME 15 minutes, plus 10 minutes inactive time
COOK TIME 50 minutes

I grew up enjoying this classic casserole. Traditionally, it is made with ground lamb, but I find that ground beef works equally well and is a little milder for young palates. You can cook everything in one dish for easy cleanup, which is a plus.

1 cup dried diced Potatoes (page 95)

1 quart low-sodium chicken broth, divided

1 tablespoon butter

½ teaspoon sea salt, divided

1 pound lean ground beef

½ cup dried diced Onions (page 92)

½ cup dried diced Carrots (page 76)

½ cup dried Peas (page 93)

2 dried cloves of Garlic (page 82), ground to a fine powder

1 tablespoon dried sliced Tomatoes (page 98), ground to a fine powder

1 teaspoon dried rosemary (see Herbs: Perennial, page 87)

1 teaspoon dried thyme (see Herbs: Perennial, page 87)

Freshly ground black pepper

1. In a medium saucepan over medium-low heat, combine the potatoes and 2 cups of the chicken broth. Cover and bring to a simmer. Cook for about 20 minutes until the potatoes are tender and most of the liquid has been absorbed. Remove from the heat. With a potato masher, mash the potatoes until smooth. Stir in the butter. Season with ¼ teaspoon of the sea salt.

2. Preheat the oven to 400°F.

3. Heat a large skillet over medium heat. Brown the ground beef, stirring, just until no longer pink, about 5 minutes.

4. Stir in the remaining ¼ teaspoon sea salt, the onions, carrots, peas, garlic powder, tomato powder, rosemary, and thyme. Season with pepper.

5. Stir in the remaining 2 of cups chicken broth. Cook for 10 minutes until some of the liquid has been absorbed and the vegetables begin to soften. Pour the mixture into an 8-by-8-inch baking dish.

6. Spread the mashed potatoes over the ground beef mixture. Bake for 20 minutes, or until the potatoes are gently browned.

7. Let rest for 10 minutes before serving.

PER SERVING CALORIES: 318; FAT: 11G; CARBS: 16G; SUGAR: 4G; FIBER: 3G; PROTEIN: 38G; SODIUM: 413MG

Cabbage & Beef Stew

YIELD 4 servings ❋ PREP TIME 5 minutes ❋ COOK TIME 1½ to 2 hours

The comforting flavors of beef, potatoes, and cabbage have a hearty "old country" feel to them. If you prefer a low-carb version, replace the potatoes with additional cabbage or simply omit them.

1 tablespoon coconut oil

1 pound beef chuck, cut into 1-inch cubes

Sea salt

Freshly ground black pepper

1 cup dried shredded Cabbage (page 75)

1 cup dried diced Potatoes (page 95)

¼ cup dried diced Celery (page 78)

¼ cup dried diced Onions (page 92)

1 teaspoon dried thyme
(see Herbs: Perennial, page 87)

1 teaspoon dried marjoram
(see Herbs: Perennial, page 87)

1 quart low-sodium beef broth

1. In a large pot over medium-high heat, heat the coconut oil.

2. Pat the beef cubes dry with paper towels. Season well with sea salt and pepper. Add them to the pan and brown for 1 to 2 minutes on each side. You may need to do this in batches so as not to crowd the pan.

3. Add the cabbage, potatoes, celery, onions, thyme, and marjoram.

4. Stir in the beef broth until everything is combined. Cover and bring to a simmer over medium-low heat. Cook for 1½ to 2 hours until the meat and vegetables are tender. Adjust the seasonings and serve.

PER SERVING CALORIES: 338; FAT: 11G; CARBS: 19G; SUGAR: 2G; FIBER: 4G; PROTEIN: 37G; SODIUM: 210MG

Mushroom and Rosemary–Crusted Beef Tenderloin

YIELD 4 servings ❋ PREP TIME 10 minutes ❋ COOK TIME 50 minutes to 1 hour

Dried mushrooms add umami flavor and surprising complexity to this basic roasted beef tenderloin. Serve with mashed potatoes and steamed vegetables.

1 (1½-pounds) center-cut beef tenderloin

1 tablespoon extra-virgin olive oil

¼ cup dried sliced Mushrooms (page 91), ground to a fine powder

1 dried clove of Garlic (page 82), ground to a fine powder

1 tablespoon dried rosemary (see Herbs: Perennial, page 87)

¼ teaspoon sea salt

Freshly ground black pepper

1. Preheat the oven to 400°F.

2. Pat the beef tenderloin dry with paper towels. Coat it with the olive oil.

3. In a small bowl, mix the mushroom powder, garlic powder, rosemary, and sea salt. Season with pepper. Coat the tenderloin with the mushroom and herb mixture.

4. Place the meat on a rimmed baking sheet. Roast for 50 minutes to 1 hour, uncovered, or until the beef is cooked through (to an internal temperature 135° to 145°F).

5. Let the beef rest for 10 minutes before slicing and serving.

PER SERVING CALORIES: 394; FAT: 21G; CARBS: 1G; SUGAR: 0G; FIBER: 0G; PROTEIN: 47G; SODIUM: 222MG

Meatballs with Italian Herbed Marinara

YIELD 4 servings ❀ PREP TIME 15 minutes, plus 30 minutes inactive time
COOK TIME 30 minutes

I'm such a fan of juicy meatballs submerged in an herbed marinara sauce. Serve with pasta, if you like, or enjoy them just like this for a complete meal that's naturally low in carbs.

FOR THE MEATBALLS

1 pound lean ground beef

1 egg, beaten

¼ cup bread crumbs

¼ cup dried diced Onions (page 92)

½ teaspoon dried oregano
  (see Herbs: Perennial, page 87)

½ teaspoon dried thyme
  (see Herbs: Perennial, page 87)

½ teaspoon dried rosemary
  (see Herbs: Perennial, page 87)

⅛ teaspoon sea salt

Freshly ground black pepper

2 tablespoons extra-virgin olive oil

FOR THE MARINARA SAUCE

2 cups low-sodium vegetable broth

1 cup dried sliced Tomatoes (page 98)

¼ cup dried diced Onions (page 92)

1 dried clove of Garlic (page 82)

1 teaspoon dried oregano
  (see Herbs: Perennial, page 87)

1 teaspoon dried thyme
  (see Herbs: Perennial, page 87)

1 teaspoon dried rosemary
  (see Herbs: Perennial, page 87)

⅛ teaspoon sea salt

To make the meatballs

1. In a medium bowl, mix the ground beef, egg, bread crumbs, onions, oregano, thyme, rosemary, and sea salt. Season with pepper.

2. Form the mixture into balls about the size of golf balls. Set them on a tray and refrigerate for at least 30 minutes or up to overnight to allow the flavors to blend and the onions to soften.

To make the marinara sauce

1. While the meatballs rest, in a small saucepan over medium-low heat, combine the vegetable broth, tomatoes, onions, garlic, oregano, thyme, rosemary, and sea salt. Bring to a simmer. Cook for about 20 minutes, stirring occasionally, until the tomatoes are very tender.

2. Transfer half of the tomato mixture to a blender and purée until smooth. Return it to the pan. Continue cooking until thick and fragrant, about 5 minutes more.

To finish

1. In a large skillet over medium heat, heat the olive oil. Add the meatballs and cook for about 10 minutes, turning carefully to brown on all sides, until cooked through (to an internal temperature of 160°F).

2. Serve with the sauce.

PER SERVING CALORIES: 340; FAT: 16G; CARBS: 10G; SUGAR: 2G; FIBER: 2G; PROTEIN: 38G; SODIUM: 295MG

Desserts

Plum Compote 226

Apple-Thyme Compote
in Pinot Noir 227

Apricot & Fig Crisp 228

Strawberry-Rhubarb
Crisp 230

Vanilla-Peach Pie 231

Fig & Berry Pie 232

Cranberry Quick Bread
with Orange Glaze 234

Crêpes with Citrus-Fig
Compote 236

Apple-Cinnamon Oven
Pancakes 238

Chocolate Bark 239

Plum Compote

YIELD 2 cups ❋ PREP TIME 5 minutes ❋ COOK TIME 40 minutes

It doesn't get simpler or more exquisite than this plum compote. Since it is already quite sweet, it is best served with just a dollop of crème fraîche. For a truly decadent dessert, though, you can serve it with vanilla ice cream and biscotti.

2 cups dried Plums (page 66)

1½ cups brandy

1 cup brewed black tea

¼ cup honey or brown sugar

2 cinnamon sticks

1 teaspoon dried orange zest
(see Citrus Fruits, page 52)

1. In a medium saucepan over medium-low heat, stir together the plums, brandy, tea, honey, cinnamon sticks, and orange zest. Cover and bring to a simmer. Cook for 20 minutes.

2. Remove the lid and continue simmering for about 20 minutes until the plums are very soft and the liquid has thickened and coats the back of a spoon.

3. Remove from the heat. Let cool to room temperature before serving.

SERVING TIP: *This dish might appeal to adults more because children aren't used to the flavor of brandy.*

PER SERVING (½ CUP) CALORIES: 202; FAT: 0G; CARBS: 35G; SUGAR: 32G; FIBER: 2G; PROTEIN: 1G; SODIUM: 1MG

Apple-Thyme Compote in Pinot Noir

YIELD 2 cups * PREP TIME 5 minutes * COOK TIME 40 minutes

Apples and thyme sound like an unlikely match but are delicious and complex when paired in this simple dessert. It is divine spooned into individual ramekins and topped with a simple crumble of nuts and dates.

2 cups Pinot Noir or other light, dry red wine

2 cups dried Apples (page 46)

¼ cup honey or brown sugar

2 cinnamon sticks

1 teaspoon dried thyme (see Herbs: Perennial, page 87)

1. In a medium saucepan over medium-low heat, stir together the Pinot Noir, apples, honey, cinnamon sticks, and thyme. Cover and bring to a simmer. Cook for 20 minutes.

2. Remove the lid and continue simmering for about 20 minutes until the apples are very soft and the liquid has thickened and coats the back of a spoon. Remove and discard the cinnamon sticks.

3. Remove from the heat. Let cool to room temperature before serving.

SUBSTITUTION TIP: Consider using other savory herbs, such as rosemary, when cooking desserts.

PER SERVING (½ CUP) CALORIES: 191; FAT: 0G; CARBS: 28G; SUGAR: 24G; FIBER: 1G; PROTEIN: 0G; SODIUM: 7MG

Apricot & Fig Crisp

YIELD 6 servings ❊ PREP TIME 10 minutes, plus 1 hour inactive time
COOK TIME 45 minutes

This crisp is amazing served with a scoop of vanilla ice cream and enjoyed on a summer afternoon. Or, brighten your winter with this taste of late summer fruits. With dried foods, you can enjoy these flavors any time of year.

1½ cups dried halved Apricots
   (page 47)

1½ cups dried diced Figs (page 56)

2 cups freshly squeezed orange juice

1 cup water

1 stick butter, softened

¼ cup dried shredded Coconut
   (page 53)

½ cup old-fashioned rolled oats

½ cup whole-wheat pastry flour

¼ cup coconut palm sugar or
   brown sugar

Pinch of sea salt

1 teaspoon vanilla extract

1. In a large bowl, combine the apricots, figs, orange juice, and water. Press the fruit down to submerge it. Let sit to rehydrate for 1 hour at room temperature.

2. Preheat the oven to 350°F.

3. Grease a 2-quart baking dish with 1 teaspoon of the butter.

4. Drain the fruit and spread it in the prepared dish. Discard any excess soaking liquid.

5. In a food processor or blender, pulse the coconut, oats, flour, palm sugar, and sea salt a few times until coarsely ground.

6. Add the remaining butter and the vanilla. Pulse just until blended but still chunky. Sprinkle the topping mixture over the figs and apricots.

7. Bake for 45 minutes, or until the fruit is soft and the topping is gently browned.

NUTRITIONAL HIGHLIGHT: For a gluten-free crisp, use gluten-free oats and a gluten-free flour blend, available in health food stores and online.

PER SERVING CALORIES: 433; FAT: 20G; CARBS: 64G; SUGAR: 41G; FIBER: 8G; PROTEIN: 5G; SODIUM: 158MG

Strawberry-Rhubarb Crisp

YIELD 6 servings ❖ PREP TIME 10 minutes, plus 1 hour inactive time
COOK TIME 45 minutes

Strawberry and rhubarb are a classic combination. The strawberries brim with natural sweetness that is offset by the complexity of the rhubarb. Rehydrate them with apple juice and skip the refined sugar altogether.

2 cups dried sliced Strawberries
(page 69)

1 cup dried diced Rhubarb (page 68)

4 cups apple juice

A scant ¼ cup melted coconut oil,
plus 1 teaspoon

½ cup roughly chopped dried almonds
(see Nuts & Seeds, page 62)

½ cup dried Dates (page 55)

½ cup old-fashioned rolled oats

Pinch of sea salt

1 teaspoon vanilla extract

1. In a medium bowl, combine the strawberries and rhubarb.

2. Pour in the apple juice, pressing the fruit down to submerge it. Let sit to rehydrate for 1 hour at room temperature.

3. Preheat the oven to 350°F.

4. Grease a 2-quart baking dish with 1 teaspoon of the coconut oil.

5. Drain the fruit and spread it in the prepared dish. Discard any excess soaking liquid.

6. In a food processor or blender, pulse the almonds, dates, oats, and sea salt a few times until coarsely ground.

7. Add the remaining ¼ cup of coconut oil and the vanilla. Pulse just until blended but still chunky. Sprinkle the topping mixture over the rhubarb and strawberries.

8. Bake for 45 minutes, or until the fruit is soft and the topping is gently browned.

NUTRITIONAL HIGHLIGHT: Dates are naturally sweet so there's no need to add any sugar to this crumble.

PER SERVING CALORIES: 312; FAT: 14G; CARBS: 46G; SUGAR: 32G; FIBER: 6G; PROTEIN: 4G; SODIUM: 49MG

Vanilla-Peach Pie

YIELD 8 servings ✤ PREP TIME 5 minutes ✤ COOK TIME 1 hour

There is such a short season when peaches are ripe and dripping with the sweetness of summer. But if you preserve them at their peak, you can enjoy their goodness year-round.

8 cups water

4 cups dried sliced Peaches (page 61)

1 vanilla bean, sliced lengthwise

2 tablespoons honey

1 tablespoon cold butter

1 box purchased pastry crusts (2 crusts)

1. In a large saucepan over medium-low heat, place the water, peaches, and vanilla bean halves. Bring to a simmer. Cook for 10 to 15 minutes, or until the peaches are barely tender.

2. Preheat the oven to 350°F.

3. Line a standard 9-inch pie plate with one piecrust.

4. With a slotted spoon, transfer the peaches onto the piecrust.

5. Continue simmering the soaking liquid and vanilla bean until reduced to just a few tablespoons. Remove from the heat. Stir in the honey.

6. Drizzle the vanilla-honey syrup over the peaches. Dot with the butter.

7. Top the peaches with the remaining piecrust and crimp the edges to seal. Make a few slits in the top crust to allow steam to escape.

8. Bake for 45 to 55 minutes until the top is gently browned. Serve warm or at room temperature.

SUBSTITUTION TIP: This pie is also delicious made with apples. Simply replace the vanilla bean with 1 teaspoon cinnamon and $\frac{1}{2}$ teaspoon nutmeg.

PER SERVING CALORIES: 213; FAT: 12G; CARBS: 25G; SUGAR: 10G; FIBER: 1G; PROTEIN: 2G; SODIUM: 215 MG

Fig & Berry Pie

YIELD 8 servings ✽ PREP TIME 20 minutes, plus 8 hours inactive time
COOK TIME 45 to 55 minutes

Making pie with frozen berries often results in an excess amount of liquid and a soggy crust. Dried berries eliminate this problem and produce a dense, sweet filling you'll love!

1½ cups dried Blueberries (page 50)

1 cups dried Cherries (page 51)

1 cup dried Figs (page 56)

6 cups apple juice

1 box purchased pastry crust (1 crust)

1 teaspoon dried lemon zest
  (see Citrus Fruits, page 52)

1 tablespoon cold butter, cut into dice

1. In a large bowl, combine the blueberries, cherries, figs, and apple juice. Refrigerate for 8 hours to rehydrate.

2. Preheat the oven to 350°F.

3. Line a standard 9-inch pie plate with the piecrust.

4. With a slotted spoon, transfer the fruit onto the piecrust.

5. Pour the remaining soaking liquid into a small saucepan. Place the pan over medium-low heat. Add the lemon zest. Bring to a simmer. Cook until only a few tablespoons of liquid remain. Drizzle this syrup over the fruit.

6. Dot the fruit with the butter. Crimp the edges of the piecrust or fold inward over the edge of the fruit.

7. Bake for 45 to 55 minutes until the top is gently browned. Serve warm or at room temperature.

PER SERVING CALORIES: 294; FAT: 7G; CARBS: 58G; SUGAR: 43G; FIBER: 5G; PROTEIN: 2G; SODIUM: 121MG

Cranberry Quick Bread with Orange Glaze

YIELD 12 slices ✷ PREP TIME 10 minutes ✷ COOK TIME 55 to 65 minutes

I love how easy it is to whip up quick breads and how adaptable they are to a variety of flavors and ingredients. For a lower sugar version, omit the orange glaze.

FOR THE GLAZE

½ cup confectioners' sugar

1 tablespoon extra-virgin olive oil

1 tablespoon freshly squeezed
orange juice

1 tablespoon dried orange zest
(see Citrus Fruits, page 52)

FOR THE BREAD

2 cups whole-wheat pastry flour

1½ teaspoons baking powder

½ teaspoon baking soda

½ teaspoon sea salt

1 cup 2% milk

¾ cup honey

¼ cup canola oil

2 large eggs

2 cups dried Cranberries (page 54)

1 tablespoon dried orange zest
(see Citrus Fruits, page 52)

To make the glaze

In a small bowl, whisk the confectioners' sugar, olive oil, orange juice, and orange zest. Set aside.

To make the bread

1. Preheat the oven to 350°F.

2. Line a 9-by-5-inch loaf pan with parchment paper. Set aside.

3. In a large bowl, combine the flour, baking powder, baking soda, and sea salt.

4. In a separate large bowl, gently beat together the milk, honey, canola oil, and eggs to combine.

5. Add the milk mixture to the flour mixture, stirring just until mixed.

6. Fold in the cranberries and orange zest.

7. Pour the batter into the prepared pan. Bake for 55 to 65 minutes, or until a toothpick inserted in the center comes out clean.

8. Allow to cool completely on a rack, for about 10 minutes.

9. Stir the glaze and drizzle it over the cooled bread. Let the glaze set for 5 minutes before slicing.

PER SERVING (1 SLICE) CALORIES: 244; FAT: 7G; CARBS: 42G; SUGAR: 24G; FIBER: 1G; PROTEIN: 4G; SODIUM: 153MG

Crêpes with Citrus-Fig Compote

YIELD 12 servings ❈ PREP TIME 10 minutes ❈ COOK TIME 20 minutes

Citrus and figs are a delicious combination. They make an especially delicious dessert or brunch when served over crêpes.

FOR THE COMPOTE

1 cup freshly squeezed orange juice

1 cup water

1 cup sliced dried Figs (page 56)

1 teaspoon dried orange zest (see Citrus Fruits, page 52)

FOR THE CRÊPES

2 large eggs

1 cup milk

3 tablespoons melted butter, plus more at room temperature for cooking the crêpes

1 tablespoon honey

1 teaspoon vanilla extract

1 cup all-purpose flour

Pinch of sea salt

To make the compote

In a small saucepan over medium-low heat, stir together the orange juice, water, figs, and orange zest. Bring to a simmer. Cook for 15 minutes until the figs are softened and the liquid is reduced by half.

To make the crêpes

1. In a blender, pulse the eggs, milk, the melted butter, honey, vanilla, flour, and sea salt until smooth, scraping down the sides of the bowl once or twice. Let rest for 10 minutes.

2. While the compote cooks down, heat a small skillet over medium heat.

3. When hot, melt about 1 teaspoon of the butter at room temperature. Swirl to coat the pan. When the butter is bubbling, pour about 2 tablespoons of batter into the pan. Swirl the pan to spread the batter.

4. Cook the crêpe for about 1 minute until barely set. Shake the pan and flip the crêpe. Cook the other side for about 15 seconds. Slide the crêpe out onto a warmed plate.

5. Repeat with the remaining batter, adding more butter as needed.

6. Serve with the warm compote.

COOKING TIP: Make sure to let the crêpe batter rest for 10 minutes before cooking the crêpes; it helps them hold together better.

PER SERVING (2 CRÊPES) CALORIES: 143; FAT: 4G; CARBS: 23G; SUGAR: 12G; FIBER: 2G; PROTEIN: 4G; SODIUM: 64MG

Apple-Cinnamon Oven Pancakes

YIELD 8 servings ❊ PREP TIME 5 minutes, plus 10 minutes inactive time
COOK TIME 15 minutes

This dish makes an equally good breakfast or dessert. I love the way the eggs puff up high in the pan. Serve with whipped butter or a small scoop of vanilla ice cream.

6 large eggs

1 cup 2% milk

1 tablespoon honey

1 teaspoon vanilla extract

1 cup all-purpose flour

1 teaspoon cinnamon

½ teaspoon freshly grated nutmeg

¼ teaspoon sea salt

2 cups dried sliced Apples (page 46)

1 teaspoon butter

1. In a blender, pulse the eggs, milk, honey, and vanilla a few times.

2. Add the flour, cinnamon, nutmeg, and sea salt. Pulse a few times, then scrape down the sides of the bowl and blend for just 2 to 3 seconds.

3. Stir in the dried apples. Let the batter rest for 10 minutes.

4. Preheat the oven to 425°F.

5. Lightly grease a 2-quart baking dish with the butter.

6. Pour the batter into the prepared baking dish. Bake for 15 minutes, or until the pancake is puffed and golden.

SUBSTITUTION TIP: To make these pancakes gluten-free, use a gluten-free flour blend such as Cup4Cup or Bob's Red Mill 1-to-1 Baking Flour.

PER SERVING CALORIES: 156; FAT: 5G; CARBS: 20G; SUGAR: 5G; FIBER: 1G; PROTEIN: 8G; SODIUM: 131MG

Chocolate Bark

YIELD 24 pieces ❋ PREP TIME 10 minutes ❋ COOK TIME 10 minutes

Don't be intimidated by the process of melting chocolate. Once you get the hang of it, you can wow your friends with smooth, glossy chocolate confections. Bonus, because you're cooking, you can omit many of the unfriendly ingredients present in purchased chocolates. Choose baking chocolate, not a ready-to-eat bar, which may contain wax.

1 pound chocolate, cocoa 70% minimum, divided

½ cup dried Cranberries (page 54)

½ cup dried Blueberries (page 50)

½ cup dried pecans (see Nuts & Seeds, page 62)

½ cup roughly chopped dried almonds (see Nuts & Seeds, page 62)

1. In a heatproof bowl over a pot filled with 1 inch of barely simmering water, place ⅔ pound of the chocolate. Allow it to melt for about 5 minutes undisturbed, or until more than half of it is melted.

2. While the chocolate is melting, line a baking sheet with parchment paper and prepare the remaining ingredients.

3. As the chocolate begins to melt, gently stir it with a spatula until it is completely melted and hot. Touch the spatula to your inner wrist. The chocolate should feel unpleasantly hot to the touch. Quickly transfer the bowl to a heatproof work surface. Stir in the remaining ⅓ pound of chocolate until melted.

4. Spread the melted chocolate onto the prepared baking sheet. You do not need to spread it to the edges, but simply to the desired thickness. Sprinkle the chocolate with the cranberries, blueberries, pecans, and almonds.

5. Place the pan in a cool place and let the chocolate set. Once hardened, break into pieces and serve.

6. Store leftovers in an airtight container in a cool place.

SUBSTITUTION TIP: Use whatever combination of fruit and nuts you enjoy. Try shredded coconut and walnuts for a German chocolate style or dried cherries and almonds.

PER SERVING (2 PIECES) CALORIES: 239; FAT: 14G; CARBS: 24G; SUGAR: 21G; FIBER: 2G; PROTEIN: 4G; SODIUM: 30MG

The Dirty Dozen & The Clean Fifteen

A nonprofit and environmental watchdog organization called the Environmental Working Group (EWG) looks at data supplied by the U.S. Department of Agriculture (USDA) and the Food and Drug Administration (FDA) about pesticide residues. Each year it compiles a list of the lowest and highest pesticide loads found in commercial crops. You can use these lists to decide which fruits and vegetables to buy organic to minimize your exposure to pesticides and which produce is considered safe enough to buy conventionally. This does not mean they are pesticide-free, though, so wash these fruits and vegetables thoroughly.

These lists change every year, so make sure you look up the most recent one before you fill your shopping cart. You'll find the most recent lists as well as a guide to pesticides in produce at EWG.org/FoodNews.

THE DIRTY DOZEN	THE CLEAN FIFTEEN
Apples	Asparagus
Celery	Avocados
Cherry tomatoes	Cabbage
Cucumbers	Cantaloupes (domestic)
Grapes	Cauliflower
Nectarines (imported)	Eggplants
Peaches	Grapefruits
Potatoes	Kiwis
Snap peas (imported)	Mangos
Spinach	Onions
Strawberries	Papayas
Sweet bell peppers	Pineapples
	Sweet corn
* Kale/Collard greens	Sweet peas (frozen)
Hot peppers	Sweet potatoes

* In addition to the dirty dozen, the EWG added two produce contaminated with highly toxic organo-phosphate insecticides.

Measurement Conversion Tables

VOLUME EQUIVALENTS (LIQUID)

US STANDARD	US STANDARD (OUNCES)	METRIC (APPROXIMATE)
2 tablespoons	1 fl. oz.	30 mL
¼ cup	2 fl. oz.	60 mL
½ cup	4 fl. oz.	120 mL
1 cup	8 fl. oz.	240 mL
1½ cups	12 fl. oz.	355 mL
2 cups or 1 pint	16 fl. oz.	475 mL
4 cups or 1 quart	32 fl. oz.	1 L
1 gallon	128 fl. oz.	4 L

OVEN TEMPERATURES

FAHRENHEIT (F)	CELSIUS (C) (APPROXIMATE)
250°F	120°C
300°F	150°C
325°F	165°C
350°F	180°C
375°F	190°C
400°F	200°C
425°F	220°C
450°F	230°C

VOLUME EQUIVALENTS (DRY)

US STANDARD	METRIC (APPROXIMATE)
¼ teaspoon	1 mL
½ teaspoon	2 mL
1 teaspoon	5 mL
1 tablespoon	15 mL
¼ cup	59 mL
⅓ cup	79 mL
½ cup	118 mL
1 cup	177 mL

WEIGHT EQUIVALENTS

US STANDARD	METRIC (APPROXIMATE)
½ ounce	15 g
1 ounce	30 g
2 ounces	60 g
4 ounces	115 g
8 ounces	225 g
12 ounces	340 g
16 ounces or 1 pound	455 g

References

BOOKS

Axcell, Claudia, Vikki Kinmont Kath, and Diana Cooke. *Simple Foods for the Pack*. San Francisco: Sierra Club Books, 2004.

Bell, Mary. *Mary Bell's Complete Dehydrator Cookbook*. New York: HarperCollins, 1994.

Marrone, Teresa. *The Beginner's Guide to Making and Using Dried Foods*. North Adams, MA: Storey, 2014.

Melngailis, Sarma. *Living Raw Food*. New York: William Morrow, 2009.

WEBSITES

Colorado State University Extension. "Cost of Preserving and Storing Food." Accessed December 12, 2015. extension.colostate.edu/topic-areas/nutrition-food -safety-health/cost-of-preserving-and-storing-food-8-704/.

Dehydrator Judge. "Best Food Dehydrator Reviews." Accessed December 10, 2015. dehydratorjudge.com/a-brief-history-of-food-drying/.

Kansas Historical Society. "Food Preservation." Accessed December 8, 2015. www.kshs.org/kansapedia/food-preservation/17877.

Outdoor Herbivore Blog. "Nutrient Losses in Dried Foods." Accessed December 12, 2015. blog.outdoorherbivore.com/food-301/nutrient-loss-in-dried-foods/.

United States Department of Agriculture, SNAP-Ed Connection. "Nutrition Through the Seasons." Food Preservation Tips and Resources. Accessed January 20, 2016. snaped.fns.usda.gov/nutrition-through-seasons/food-preservation-tips-and -resources.

Food and Equipment

FOOD

Equal Exchange Baking Cocoa

equalexchange.coop

Available online at many retailers, such as Amazon.com.

Gluten-Free Flour

Bob's Red Mill 1-to-1 Baking Flour

www.bobsredmill.com/gluten-free-1-to-1-baking-flour.html

Cup4Cup

For store locator

www.cup4cup.com

EQUIPMENT

Microplane Grater

us.microplane.com/microplanekitchentools.aspx

ParaFlexx Drying Sheets by Excalibur

www.excaliburdehydrator.com/dehydration-accessories/drying-sheets

Recipe Index

A

Apple-Cinnamon Fruit
Leather, 116
Apple-Cinnamon Oven
Pancakes, 238
Apple-Thyme Compote
in Pinot Noir, 227
Apricot & Fig Crisp, 228
Apricot Chicken with
Rosemary, 204

B

Basic Chicken Jerky, 108
Basic Energy Bars, 122
Basic Nut Crackers, 133
Basic Venison Jerky, 111
Berry Blast Smoothie, 153
Berry Lover's Trail Mix, 120
Berry-Almond Granola, 159
Borscht, 178
Breakfast Crêpes, 135
Broccoli-Cheddar Bisque, 177

C

Cabbage & Beef Stew, 220
Carrot-Ginger-Orange Soup, 182
Cauliflower Fritters with
Shallots & Balsamic
Syrup, 139
Chicken Skewers Agrodolce
with Dried Figs, 207
Chocolate Bark, 239
Chocolate-Orange
Energy Bars, 123
Classic Beef Jerky, 104
Coconut Macaroons, 125
Corn Chowder, 171
Corn Fritters, 197
Cranberry Quick Bread with
Orange Glaze, 234–235

Cream of Celery Soup, 175
Cream of Mushroom Soup, 174
Cream of Tomato Soup, 169
Creamy Cauliflower Soup, 177
Crêpes with Citrus-Fig
Compote, 236–237

D

Duck Jerky, 110

E

Eggplant, Zucchini & Spinach
Lasagna, 198–199

F

Falafel, 140
Fig & Berry Pie, 232
Fish Jerky, 113
French Onion Soup, 172
Fruity Quinoa Pilaf, 164
Fudgy Chocolate-Cherry
Brownies, 146

G

Ginger-Pear Fruit Leather, 118
Ginger-Soy Chicken
Jerky, 109
Grain-Free Fruit &
Nut Granola, 160
Ground Beef Jerky, 106

H

Hearty Beef Chili, 217
Herb-Crusted Pork Loin with
Cranberry Sauce, 214–215
Herbes de Provence, 88

I

Italian Herb Blend, 88

J

Juice Pulp Crackers, 132

K

Kale & White Bean Soup, 180

L

Lamb Meatballs with
Tzatziki Sauce, 208–209
Leek & Potato Soup, 183
Loaded Sweet Potato
Tacos, 196

M

Meatballs with Italian Herbed
Marinara, 222–223
Minestrone Soup, 176
Mint & Pea Soup, 170
Monkeying Around
Trail Mix, 121
Morning Glory Muffins, 158
Mushroom & Pea
Risotto, 188–189
Mushroom & Tomato
Frittata, 200
Mushroom and Rosemary-
Crusted Beef Tenderloin, 221

O

Oatmeal Raisin Cookies, 126
Onion Rings with Raw
Chipotle Aioli, 138

P

Pan-Seared Pork Chops with
Mango Chutney, 211
Pear Crisp, 129
Pineapple Fruit Leather, 119
Plantain Cakes with Raw
Sriracha, 136–137

Plum Compote, 226
Polenta with Mushrooms,
    190–191
Pork Tenderloin with
    Stewed Pears, 216
Power Greens Smoothie, 152
Pumpkin Bread, 156

R

Ratatouille, 186
Raw Flaxseed Bread, 134
Raw Spinach Fettucine with
    Tomato Cream Sauce, 144–145
Raw Veggie Pizza, 142–143
Root Vegetable Gratin, 187
Rosemary-Almond
    Crackers, 124

S

Salted Chocolate Chip
    Cookies, 128

Salted Chocolate
    Cranberry Bars, 162
Shepherd's Pie, 218
Southwestern Stuffed
    Chicken Breasts, 206
Spanish Lamb Stew, 210
Spicy Ground Beef Jerky, 107
Spicy Thai Curry, 195
Spicy Veggie Chickpea
    Burgers, 192
Strawberry-Lime Fruit
    Leather, 117
Strawberry-Rhubarb Crisp, 230
Sweet Potato Chicken
    Nachos, 205
Sweet-&-Sour Meatballs
    with Pineapple, 212–213

T

Teriyaki Beef Jerky, 105
Teriyaki Venison Jerky, 112
Tropical Breeze Smoothie, 154

V

Vanilla-Peach Pie, 231
Vanilla-Peach Slow
    Cooker Oatmeal, 163
Vegan Blueberry-Apple
    Muffins, 155
Vegetable Broth Mix, 168
Vegetarian Fried Rice, 194
Veggie Breakfast Casserole, 165

Z

Zucchini Bread, 157
Zucchini-Oregano-
    Lemon Frittata, 201

Index

A

acidulated water soaking, 35–36
agrodolce, 207
airflow and ventilation, 19
apples, dehydrating, 32, 46
apricots, dehydrating, 47
asparagus
  dehydrating, 72
  peeling, 32

B

baking cocoa, 244
bananas, dehydrating, 32, 47
beef chili, 217
beef jerky
  classic, 104
  cost savings, 17
  ground, 106
  spicy ground, 107
  teriyaki, 105
beef stew, 220
beef tenderloin, 221
beets, dehydrating, 73
blanching and shocking, 35
blender, 27
blueberries
  checking, 33
  dehydrating, 50
blueberry-apple muffins, 155
botanical herbs, dehydrating, 85
box-style dehydrator, 26
breads
  cranberry with orange
    glaze, 234–235
  pumpkin, 156
  raw flaxseed, 134
  zucchini, 157
broccoli, dehydrating, 74
broths, Vegetable
  Broth Mix, 168
brownies, 146

C

cabbage, dehydrating, 75
cabinet-style dehydrator, 26
carrots
  dehydrating, 76
  peeling, 32
cauliflower, dehydrating, 77
celery, dehydrating, 78
celery soup, 173
Celsius, Fahrenheit
  equivalent, 242
checking foods, 32
cherries, dehydrating, 51
chicken
  Apricot Chicken with
    Rosemary, 204
  Chicken Skewers Agrodolce
    with Dried Figs, 207
  food safety, 33
  Southwestern Stuffed
    Chicken Breasts, 206
  Sweet Potato Chicken
    Nachos, 205
chicken jerky
  basic, 108
  ginger-soy, 109
chickpea burgers, 192
chili, 217
chocolate chip cookies, 128
chocolate cranberry bars, 162
citrus fruits, dehydrating, 52
The Clean Fifteen, 241
cleaning and sanitizing
  equipment, 33
cleaning dehydrators, 27
cocoa for baking, 244
coconut, dehydrating, 23, 53
compote
  citrus-fig, 236–237
  Pinot Noir, thyme & apple, 227
  plum, 226

conditioning, 39
containers, 28
cookies
  oatmeal raisin, 126
  salted chocolate
    chip, 128
corn, dehydrating, 79
crackers
  basic nut, 133
  drying times, 37
  juice pulp, 132
  rosemary-almond, 124
cranberries, dehydrating, 54
cranberry bars, 162
crêpes, breakfast, 135
crispness of food, 41
crisps, apricot & fig, 228
cucumbers, dehydrating, 80
cups, measurement
  conversion tables, 242
curry, 195
cutting and slicing foods, 33
cutting boards, cleaning
  and sanitizing, 33

D

dates, dehydrating, 55
dehydrated foods.
  See also foods
  eating, 39
  grinding into powder, 39
  shelf life, 15–16
  using in cooking, 40
dehydration
  airflow and ventilation, 19
  benefits, 15–17
  foods unsuited to, 19
  and nutrients, 20
  raw material preparation, 19
  suggested foods, 32
  time and temperature, 18

dehydration methods
  electric food dehydrator
    drying, 22
  oven and convection
    oven drying, 21
  sun drying, 21
dehydrators
  cleaning, 27
  and raw food diet, 22–23
  types, 26
dessicants, 28
The Dirty Dozen, 241
doneness, determining, 38
dried foods, healthiness of, 16
dry volume equivalents, 242
drying food, history of, 14
drying times
  averages, 37
  size and surface area, 37
  sugar content, 36
  water content, 36
drying unevenly, 41
duck jerky, 110. *See also*
  food safety

E

E. coli, eliminating
  from meat, 104
eating locally, 15
eggplant, dehydrating, 81
electric food dehydrator
  drying, 22
emergency readiness, 16
energy bars
  basic, 122
  chocolate-orange, 123
  cost savings, 17
equipment and tools, 27–28, 244
EWG (Environmental
  Working Group), 241

F

Fahrenheit, Celsius
  equivalent, 242
family time, 23

FDA (Food and Drug
  Administration), 241
figs, dehydrating, 56
flavors, concentrating, 17
flaxseed bread, 134
flour, gluten-free, 244
food dehydration. *See*
  dehydration
food processor, 27
food safety, 33, 38. *See
  also* duck jerky
foods. *See also* dehydrated foods
  allowing time and space, 34
  choosing carefully, 34
  cooling, 34
  dehydrating
    simultaneously, 37
  preparing evenly, 34
  pretreating, 35–36
  rehydrating, 40
  selecting for dehydration, 32
  storing carefully, 34
  transporting, 16
fried rice, 194
frittata
  mushroom & tomato, 200
  zucchini-oregano-lemon, 201
fruit and nut granola, 160
fruit leathers
  apple-cinnamon, 116
  drying times, 37
  ginger-pear, 118
  pineapple, 119
  sticking to mat, 41
  strawberry-lime, 117
fruits
  checking, 33
  determining doneness, 38
  drying temperatures, 18
  drying times, 37

G

gallons, measurement
  conversion tables, 242
gardening, 29

garlic
  dehydrating, 82
  peeling, 32
ginger
  dehydrating, 83
  peeling, 32
gluten-free flour, 244
granola
  berry-almond, 159
  grain-free fruit & nut, 160
grapes
  checking, 33
  dehydrating, 57
green beans, dehydrating, 84
grinding foods into powders, 39

H

Herbes de Provence, 88
herbs
  botanical, 85
  cooking with, 88
  determining doneness, 38
  drying temperatures, 18
  drying times, 37
  enjoying year round, 29
  perennial, 87
  recommendations, 28
humidity, 37

J

jerky
  beef, 104–107
  chicken, 108–109
  duck, 110
  fish, 113
  venison, 111

K

kale
  chips, 17, 32
  dehydrating, 89
Kingsolver, Barbara, 15
kiwis, dehydrating, 58
knives, cleaning and
  sanitizing, 33

L

labels, 28
lamb stew, 210
lasagna, 198–199
leafy greens, dehydrating, 89
leeks, 170–173, 176, 186
    dehydrating, 90
liquid volume equivalents, 242

M

macaroons, 125
mandolines, 27
mangos, dehydrating, 59
measurement conversion
    tables, 242
meatballs
    Lamb Meatballs with
        Tzatziki Sauce, 208
    Sweet-&-Sour Meatballs
        with Pineapple, 212–213
meats
    determining doneness, 38
    drying temperatures, 18
    drying times, 37
    food safety, 33
Melngailis, Sarma, 17
melon, dehydrating, 60
mesh screens and trays, 27
methods of dehydration.
    See dehydration methods
metric conversions, 242
microplane grater, 244
moisture, removing, 21
money, saving, 15, 17
muffins
    morning glory, 158
    vegan blueberry-apple, 155
mushrooms
    dehydrating, 91
    with polenta, 190–191

N

nachos, 205
Navitas Power Snacks, 17

nectarines, dehydrating, 61
nut crackers, 22
nutrients, effect of
    dehydration on, 20
nuts and seeds
    dehydrating, 62
    soaking, 23

O

oatmeal, 163
onions, dehydrating, 92
oregano, 28
ounces, measurement
    conversion tables, 242
oven and convection
    oven drying, 21
oven temperatures, 242

P

pancakes, apple-
    cinnamon, 238
paraflexx mats, 27
pasteurization, 38
pathogenic bacteria,
    eliminating from
    meat, 104
peaches, dehydrating, 32, 61
pears
    dehydrating, 32, 64
    with pork tenderloin, 216
peas
    dehydrating, 93
    Mint & Pea Soup, 170
peeling foods, 32
peppers
    dehydrating, 32, 94
    enjoying year round, 29
perennial herbs,
    dehydrating, 87
pesticide residues, 241
pH, lowering, 35
Phyo, Ani, 22
pies
    fig & berry, 232
    vanilla-peach, 231

pineapple, dehydrating, 65
Pineapple Fruit Leather, 119
Pinot Noir, Thyme &
    Apple Compote, 227
pitting foods, 32
pizza, raw veggie, 142
planning ahead, 34
plums, dehydrating, 66
pork chops, 211
pork loin, 214–215
potatoes, dehydrating, 95
poultry, food safety, 33. See
    also chicken; duck jerky
pounds, measurement
    conversion tables, 242
preparation of raw
    materials, 19, 32–33
preserving food, 14, 18
pretreating foods, 35–36
pumpkin bread, 156

Q

quarts, measurement
    conversion tables, 242
quinoa pilaf, 164

R

raspberries, dehydrating, 67
raw food diet, 22–23
raw material preparation, 19
rehydrating foods, 40
rhubarb, dehydrating, 68
risotto, 188–189
root vegetables, dehydrating,
    96. See also vegetables
rosemary, 28, 124
round stackable
    dehydrators, 26
ruler, 27

S

safety of food, 33
sanitizing and cleaning
    equipment, 33
saving money, 15, 17

seasonal gardening, 29
seeds and nuts
   dehydrating, 62
   soaking, 23
shallots, 139
shelf life of dehydrated
   food, 15–17
shocking and blanching, 35
silica gel packets, 28
silicone mats, 27
size and surface area, 37
slicing and cutting foods, 33
smoothies
   power greens, 152
   tropical breeze, 154
soups
   borscht, 178
   carrot-ginger-orange, 182
   cream of celery, 175
   cream of mushroom, 174
   cream of tomato, 169
   creamy cauliflower, 179
   French onion, 178
   kale & white bean, 180
   leek & potato, 183
   minestrone, 176
   mint & pea, 170
spice grinder, 28
spinach fettucine, 144–145
squash, dehydrating, 97
sriracha with plantain
   cakes, 136–137
steaming food, 35
storage supplies, 28
strawberries, dehydrating, 69

sugar and additives,
   controlling, 17
sugar content, 36
sugar soaking, 36, 41
sun drying, 21
sweet potatoes
   peeling, 32
   in tacos, 196
syrup blanching, 35

T

tablespoons, measurement
   conversion tables, 242
tacos, 196
teaspoons, measurement
   conversion tables, 242
temperatures for
   dehydration, 18
thyme, 28
time for dehydration, 18
tips for success, 34
tomatoes
   dehydrating, 32, 98
   enjoying year round, 29
tools and equipment, 27–28
trail mix
   berries, 120
   monkeying around, 121
transporting foods, 16
troubleshooting, 41

U

USDA (US Department
   of Agriculture), 241
utensils, cleaning and
   sanitizing, 33

V

vacuum-sealing machines, 28
vegetable peeler, 28
vegetables. *See also*
   root vegetables
   acidity in, 21
   determining doneness, 38
   drying temperatures, 18
   drying times, 37
   peeling, 32
venison jerky
   basic, 111
   teriyaki, 112
ventilation and airflow, 19
vitamins, effect of
   dehydration on, 20
volume equivalents, 242

W

waste, reducing, 16
water
   content in foods, 36
   drinking, 16, 20
weight
   equivalents, 242
   watching, 16
Whitaker, John, 22
white bean soup, 180

Z

zucchini
   bread, 157
   dehydrating, 29, 99

Acknowledgments

Special thanks to the editorial team at Callisto Media, who are a delight to work with and always bring out the best in every manuscript, especially Meg, Mary, and the design team.

Unending gratitude to my mom for raising me on a diet of healthy, whole foods. Thanks to Ani Phyo for introducing me to the beauty of raw foods.

Thanks to my husband and two sons for their willingness to polish off every batch of dehydrated foods that emerged from the kitchen during recipe testing for this book. I couldn't have done it without you!

About the Author

Pamela Ellgen is a food blogger, certified personal trainer, and author of several books on cooking, nutrition, and fitness, including *Sheet Pan Paleo* and the bestselling *Healthy Slow Cooker Cookbook*. Her work has been published in *Huffington Post*, LIVESTRONG, *Darling* magazine, and Spinning.com. She lives in California with her husband and two sons. When she's not in the kitchen, she enjoys practicing yoga, surfing, and exploring the local farmers' market.

CPSIA information can be obtained
at www.ICGtesting.com
Printed in the USA
BVHW06s1340130918
527024BV00002B/2/P

9 781943 451326